AF797750

REWIRING YOUR SUCCESS

REWIRING YOUR SUCCESS

The 20 Most Powerful Secrets of Successful People

John Qreshi

Copyright ©2020 by John Qreshi
All rights reserved.

No part of this book may be reproduced in any form whatsoever, whether by graphic, visual, electronic, film, microfilm, tape recording or any other means, without prior written permission of the publisher, except in the case of brief passages embodied in critical reviews and articles.

ISBN: 978-0-578-63223-0

Published by John Qreshi Training & Research Inc.

Printed in the United States of America

You know how it is, you pick up a book, flip to the dedication and find that yet again, the author has dedicated a book to someone else, not you.

Not this time.

This one is for you... with you.
Know that,
and you probably know why.

CONTENTS

"Tough times never last but tough people do."

- Robert H. Schuller

Author's Note

When I was broke and learning how to make money online, one night an old man appeared on my computer screen, dressed in a very bright, expensive suit. He said to me from the screen, "What do you want?

What do you *really* want?" And I was hooked ... on everything from his suit to his message. His name was Bob Proctor, and I have been following him for the last fourteen years of my life.

Before this encounter, I was reading *Think and Grow Rich*, watching *The Secret,* and all that, like everyone else. Back then, I figured if I simply thought about what I wanted, that it would fall into my lap ... even though I was getting nowhere this way.

From the moment I saw Bob, however, I became immersed in not only his work, but through him, became obsessed with the work of Napoleon Hill and Earl Nightingale as well. I have since been on a path of learning all about the nature of the mind while applying it to my own life, and have since found nothing but success. Today, I am in shock and awe at how little I once saw and knew, compared to all that I know now.

It is impossible for me to put everything I've learned and experienced into one little book, especially while simplifying it for mass consumption, but I wanted to keep this book focused on the Secrets of the 1%. If you follow it, you will walk *the* pathway to succeeding in **your career.**

I've designed this book in such a way that — whether you are an entrepreneur, an employee, you don't have a job, or you don't yet know what you want — if you follow this, you will come through a very bright end of the tunnel in your own life.

Introduction

We only have two commodities in this life: **Time** and **Energy**.

I am grateful to you for taking the time and the energy to read this book. I know just how valuable our time and energy are to us all, as I have spent countless hours in loving pursuit of solving the problem this book addresses, for you.

Because of my failures, however, I know my successes well.

I have used the hours I floated through my youth to motivate me to forge for you —through so much time and energy spent learning, crafting, and polishing — an offering of the highest value.

Rest assured, if you follow and read this book thoroughly, it will become your bible of success. Some parts of the success equation I've formulated may look all too simple at first, but they are far from it. The content and concepts I offer you are part of the deep work of change, and though simple, are far from easy to implement.

You may need to read through the book a second time to truly absorb and implement the practices I offer. It will all make sense once you are able to apply and live the concepts yourself … once you can feel the difference firsthand.

And so it is: We were all born dumb, naked, and speechless. All we were given in life is a body, an empty mind, time to exist, and energy to access. We receive nothing else in this life to work with.

There is good news and bad news here. These being our only commodities, some will see this as a limitation, and others, well, will see it as freedom.

You see, you decide where to direct the energy you experience. You decide what to do with the time you have.

If you utilize your time and energy appropriately, you can do anything. Just like the cliché, I'm sure you've heard it, about how *Bill Gates has the same amount of time in a day that you do, so what's stopping you?*

Well, this is exactly what I want to help you to see clearly for yourself. So you can live the truth of the cliché, and use your mind to think like the Bill Gates of the world do. So you can win at life in whatever way that looks for you.

Maybe you aren't looking for the kind of money Gates has. Perhaps your vision of richness is lush green pastures to live on, a large family, or an executive-level position.

Whatever abundance looks like to you, we can get you there. Together, let us now embark on a journey of uncovering how to make your time and energy work for your success.

PART ONE

"You are the only problem you will ever have and you are the only solution. Change is inevitable, personal growth is always a personal decision."

- Bob Proctor

ONE

What's The Story You're Telling Yourself?

I was born and raised in a communist country.

I will get back to that later.

Living there, I was constantly surrounded by the limiting beliefs that if I didn't have a college degree, didn't go to Harvard, didn't make the right connections, I could never be successful … Pretty much, the status quo was that no matter what, I wouldn't be good enough for success.

These stories were passed down through generations, and my parents perpetuated them like any other.

I appropriated their stories, of course, and then carried their losing mindset with me as I moved forward in my life — even after leaving the communist country where I'd grown up!

I judged everything. And as a result, I lost out on connecting with people, I lost out on opportunities, and I lost out on living my best life. Before I even met someone, I'd have cultivated a laundry list of judgments about them and why I needed to be cautious. Why *they* were wrong, why *they* were to blame, and why I was, therefore, in the clear.

I used judgment as a way to keep a safe distance, not get too involved, and ensure I wouldn't get "hurt" on the way to living my best life. Thing is, I also never put both feet into anything enough to commit wholly, because my judgments were keeping me from committing.

And the worst thing about it is, really, that the judgments were just projections of my own insecurities. How else could I have seen their flaws so quickly, if I hadn't already been so deeply familiar with them in myself?

These projections showed exactly the story I was telling myself. Day in and day out. These stories, these insecurities I'd picked up and put on were so deeply instilled in my unconscious mind, however, that I wasn't able to see the story consciously … well, not for a very long time, at least.

We all tell stories. To ourselves and to the world. And we pick them up in ways we often can't consciously see.

Do you know the steps you need to take toward your goals, know the things you need to do, but you just can't get the motivation to do them? Do you hope, dream, and pray for things, but you never seem to be quite able to obtain or achieve them? Do you start making progress towards your dreams, only to sabotage the opportunities for yourself?

Why *is* this? This is the question.

Once upon a time, I read the book *Think and Grow Rich*, but there was far too much thinking and not enough growing! Nothing happened because there was no *action* to back up the mindset.

There are so many mindset books and gurus out there, but without the right understanding of how to fully shift the paradigm you're living, no impact is made! [We'll get into paradigms shortly.]

In fact, I've read *so many* books and witnessed so many gurus talk about their pathway to success, but I've never seen the results work out because they're not approaching the work from the right angle!

So then *why* is it that when you have a goal, make progress towards reaching that goal, and get halfway there or even closer, it all falls apart?

Why do we all dream for things, and put in all this extra work to try and achieve them, only for them to come crashing down, our hearts along with them?

Why is it that we're constantly involved in this dance between who we are and who we want to become?

Why? Why can't we more easily achieve the things we want to achieve?!?

Why does it have to all be so hard? *Why* do some people look like they've discovered the secret to it all, but you just can't seem to?

And *why oh why* is it you feel so alone in all this?

Does it feel like something is holding YOU back? Perhaps some invisible force or something that happened to you or didn't happen to you in your life?

What is it? And *who* is to blame?

I'm sure you've come close to these thoughts and feelings at some point in your life. And maybe that's exactly what brought you here, to this book, right now!

Well, the solution: The answer to these questions and those like them is that it's *not* just about knowing the information, or hearing someone else describe their process. And it isn't all about the tactics or tools.

There's something else. Something else that the experts and gurus haven't been talking about, for no other reason than that they haven't understood it. It hasn't yet been illuminated as the key to the puzzle.

What it all comes down to is *shifting your paradigm.*

A person's frame of reference will determine what they observe.

Your frame of reference is basically your paradigm, and is made up of all of your beliefs. It's the way you believe things to be. And this belief sculpts the way you see the world; it shapes how you perceive reality.

It's everything to you. Your paradigm is how you walk through the world and exist. And it directly affects *how* you perceive *what* you experience.

A paradigm is likely the most influential thing a human being has. Yet, most people don't know what it is, or even what the word "paradigm" means.

As humans, we tend to believe that everyone else thinks as we do. We believe that others understand what we mean when we communicate, and that we're all operating under the same rules of reality. We think that if we believe something to be true, everyone else must also.

This isn't true, however. We each perceive reality in our own way. And there is a definitive difference between how the "successful" and "unsuccessful" people think, see, believe, and act in the world.

Let me tell you more about how this all began for me. Through sharing my own personal story, you can hopefully get a real understanding of how this plays out …

I was born in a small town in the communist country of Saudi Arabia. My parents each stem from different countries, one from India and the other from Pakistan.

Because my parents were from different backgrounds, from birth until the age of seven, I wasn't raised with any sort of religion or spirituality. And because we were so poor, I was also raised with loads of limiting beliefs.

See, my parents had enough money to support my older brothers in becoming doctors, but once it was my turn through the stile, our family started experiencing extreme financial hardship. My parents couldn't support me in any sort of educational path.

This is about when I started losing interest in school. I saw no value in working so hard for no future. But I also saw clearly how the real purpose of school was to learn one thing: the difference between what is and isn't important.

The knowledge you acquire in school is a process in and of itself, but it doesn't do anything for you, or really provide you with anything. It doesn't teach you how to do your taxes, how to pay your credit card, or how to run a business … No, school was designed to guide you towards finding a job, all so you can continue to live your life, work for someone else's dream, and all the while, allow others to decide how much you should earn.

This, in fact, reminds me of something my mentor Earl Nightingale is known for saying: "Most people tiptoe their way through life, hoping they make it safely to death."

Well, living with the programmed belief that I had no choices other than to work as a slave for someone else, I saw no point in school. I received poor grades anyways, so I dropped out with the hopes of getting a job to help my parents make ends meet.

As it turned out, I got a job working at a small agency, quite literally as a Tea Boy who assisted, cleaned and served the other workers. As I was working there, the owner decided to stop paying me and the other workers, so I was working without making any money for literally four months. In other words, I was, in fact, working as a slave.

I decided after a while that I'd had enough, and quit to try something else.

I was dating a girl at this time, who thought it would be good work for us to both become spiritual advisors. I started working online as a spiritual advisor when my bank account was frozen, and I was flagged to leave the country for being an entrepreneur in my early twenties.

I was sweating and scared when I met someone who was working as a third-party agent for the United Nations. They helped me move to France, where, upon arrival, I experienced a total culture shock. The sheer difference in lifestyle knocked me off my feet.

I struggled to find residence in France, and since Europe was so big, I quickly made my way to Italy, where I lived for almost two years.

I wasn't lucky enough to get permanent status in Italy, even after having gone through a few scams where people told me that, in exchange for money, the Pope would come to the local church and grant me residency.

Hey, I was desperate and doing what I could to figure things out! I was working pretty successfully as a spiritual advisor online, but I still wanted to find a home where I could put down roots. You know, have something to build upon.

While in Italy, I encountered many people who gave me dirty looks and said, "Go back to your home country!" I would get nervous and a little scared, but after a while I just started laughing, saying to myself, "Yeah? *Which* home country?!?"

Eventually, I found these two lawyers, who were also twins, and they helped me move to and get residency in Budapest, Hungary. I still had to update my residency and report myself every three months to immigration, meaning I had to report to my landlord or they would evict me ... This was pretty scary, and I had no certainty, but I was grateful for what I had figured out and the roots I had been able to make by this point.

Slowly, I started to see success in my career sector. In early 2012, my business started to pick up nicely, to where my spiritual coaching business became full-time, and I was starting to see clear results with my clients. For a moment, I felt meaning in my life by solving problems. Not only for my clients but in the marketplace as a whole.

This motivated me and started to wake up every cell in my body that had gone cold, as a real entrepreneurial spirit started to build from within. I began to dig in even deeper to research, study, and enhance my abilities to better serve my clients and produce real change.

It was when I moved to New York City that I truly witnessed the rough and tumble competitiveness of the marketplace. I could have let this strike fear in my heart, and of course, it took a moment to find my stride, but once I did, I became fully immersed — day and night — in learning all I could.

I was helping people, but what I really wanted was to give them the Magic Pill that would unequivocally lead to powerful results. I had a lot of questions and got to work on configuring the answers. I started traveling from conference to conference, taking one course after another, hopping from one mastermind to the next, until I had racked up a total of $864,000 spent on these experiences.

In researching, studying, and developing a solid, bulletproof roadmap to solve any problem, I eventually opened up a new company, where I would craft original content for my clients to use in building their dream life. It was at this point when I started seeing *massive* results directly from my Business Coaching & Consulting services.

I was pondering the idea of sharing my ideas and research with large audiences in an effort to create a movement where people everywhere could have a solid, bulletproof, recession-proof business model, when I was warned by my peers not to share anything, except behind closed doors and only with the 1%ers.

I thought of my old self, my younger self, however. I saw myself looking for a home, feeling all that uncertainty and pain, and decided to explore the idea anyway. I ran a survey across the different conferences I was attending and platforms I was involved with and saw how, one after the other, people were all experiencing the same problems in the same pattern, while expressing frustration with not knowing exactly how to do what the gurus were doing, wondering why they couldn't share their exact processes.

This drove me insane! I couldn't *not* share what I knew after receiving these results, so I decided to launch my training and help all these people who were struggling and lost. In this moment, I was reminded of my mom. When I was young, she'd told me never to let people take advantage of me, but this is what I felt I was doing by *not* sharing what I had discovered. By letting the secrecy continue.

So I decided to do it for my mom, for those who were lost, and for my own selfish reasons. To test my full potential in life and leave a legacy, I decided to focus on a very clear mission: To create more successful entrepreneurs and allow them to see their full potential that will compound to create the greatest lift of overall global fortune.

Hey, this was the only way I could see to cut through the noise of 2 billion people on the Internet in entrepreneurship. By just being the real me and, finally, being transparent with them on how they could do what cost me a small fortune to uncover.

By the time I became a board member for The American Board of Neuro-Linguistic Programming, it had taken me three decades to truly understand that there's nothing that can be solved when we are operating from the "effect" side of life; in other words, if I am blaming others for something happening in my life, there's no way for me to actually solve the problem I'm facing.

However, if I'm operating from the "cause" side of life and see that everything I receive or experience is a representation of my own subconscious paradigm and that I alone am therefore responsible for it, I can then solve the problem head on and move along.

And yes! Of course there is a paradox in it! But once you see what's happening, you can start to observe your paradigm as it affects and shapes your own reality. This becomes especially easy when you can observe how others operate by contrast.

I, for one, came to see how — knowing this truth about the role of our paradigm in our reality — the only way I could move forward was by taking responsibility for my role in relationship to others. For the judgments I placed on others, and how those judgments were really just places where I was judging myself internally.

Realizing that my own subconscious mind was "hiring out" the people I engaged with in my life, I was able to see the projections for what they were! I am then able to know that I need not judge others or take personally what they are doing. Truly, we're all just working through the projections our paradigm illuminates.

This way of seeing how we perceive reality allows us to ask, "What is there to learn from this?"

Rather than stopping at judgment, we can seize the opportunity to grow, and we can use our paradigm to work for us in our pursuit of success, rather than against us!

In my own life, recognizing the story I was telling myself not only about others, but then too, about myself, allowed me to see that the only time I was stretching myself was when I was immersed in the continuous process of learning, unlearning, and relearning.

We are our stories. In and out. And between the ages of birth to seven, we accumulate the base programs which will create the paradigm we primarily use. We gather our stories from what we observe in our family and the world around us, including the stories we witness through media such as books, film, music, and television.

We are so attuned because we are blank canvases, ready for learning. Unfortunately, some of the situations we experience teach us habits that aren't so conducive to growth, many of which are quite damaging. And we absorb and implement them quickly and efficiently.

I was miserable in my adult life because, when I was a child, I absorbed miserable content. My parents only watched the news back then. Breaking news, at that. There wasn't much else to watch, mind you, but what was on was filled with chaos, fear, hate, and gore.

I grew up absorbed by fear and I took it with me into my adult life, where it then shaped everything I saw into a sad and somber situation.

Knowing you can choose to live from the "cause" side of life and knowing you can choose how your story continues, you can see how to take actions that facilitate *real change* in your reality.

The story I was carrying around was giving me my identity. Whatever story I was perceiving from what happened in my life was helping to shape this identity that I was not confident, that I was an introvert.

Therefore, this is who I was becoming, as it also formed a solid program in my unconscious mind. Napoleon Hill said it this way in his book: **"Our future reflects the identity we are giving to ourselves and our identity reflects the story we are telling ourselves."**

When you realize you have more of a say in how your story goes, you can see just how many small action steps you can take in your life to make things better!

Much better than if you see your life as a series of random circumstances, making you the victim, wherein you see from the "effect" perspective. In this case, there'd be no point in taking action, because you'd have no say in what happens "to you."

After researching this idea with other scientists, I have discovered that:

- The first thing to take action on is pleasure. Meaning, recognizing what you really want deep down. Not just a victim anymore. The pen's in your hand … now what do you want to write about?

  In other words, *what identity am I giving myself? How can I do this or how can I make that happen?* A question opens the mind and a statement closes the mind.

- The second thing is your environment and who you are surrounding yourself with. Your life and future has a lot to do with who you are surrounding yourself with.

- Thirdly, engagement. Being aware of what you are doing and why you are doing it. Consciousness is equal to awareness.

We don't realize just how much the media and stories affect us. We can actually use media to support rewriting the story of life we want to live. We can choose the stories to support us in narrating our stories wisely!

And indeed, we can just make it all up! We use the stories we create to craft the meaning that makes up our life when we're aware of what exactly it is we want. And then we can use this to show up in the world in a fully engaged way!

Therefore, stories are an evolutionary mechanism.

This means that because I'm living out a story that brings meaning into my life, I am more likely to work harder to not only survive but thrive. By virtue of having created the story, I've cultivated deep meaning in my life.

Now, the problem is, if it's our stories creating the meaning in our lives, once we too accept that the stories are all man-made, logically, we must accept that there is no inherent meaning to our lives. In other words, life is only as meaningful as the story we are telling.

This idea hit me pretty hard when I first came to it. I was spending all my time trying to understand what the meaning was, trying to understand how we were created, when I came to this inculpable conclusion that meaning just didn't exist … at least, not until you imbue the meaning for yourself.

Therein, actually, lies a real kind of freedom. The palpable kind. The kind we can choose to use to shape the kind of life we want to live, and from the ground up!

To create the life you want, write the story you want to read. The story which can impact not only your own life, but that of your loved ones and the other people around you.

So, now … what is the story you are telling yourself?

"The true value of a human being is determined primarily by the measure and the sense in which he has attained liberation from the self."

-Albert Einstein

TWO

The Programs Of Your Unconscious Mind

The stories we tell with our lives are the amalgamation of the programs running in our subconscious mind.

Dr. Bruce Lipton has explained in his research how 95% of our actions originate from the programs already implemented into our unconscious mind between birth and seven years old.

He explains this to be the reason poor people generally stay poor while rich people stay rich, and for most of their lives. You'll even see people who were always poor hit it big, only to end up poor again soon after.

The brain of a child under seven is in a lower vibrational frequency called theta. Theta is a state of hypnosis, where the imagination does its work. It serves as the fodder for children playing tea parties with mud pies. To them, it's the real thing. A kid rides a broom … it's a horse. It's all theta.

Before you can become conscious, your brain needs programs to run on. Otherwise, what would you even have to be conscious of? So, the first seven years are a state of preparation for becoming conscious. A state where you just watch your parents, your siblings, and your community because you have to learn.

You have to learn about the programs required to live on the planet. And how do you get them? Through theta. Through hypnosis.

Just to be a functional member of a family, and a functional member of the community, there are rules. Think about it … the hundreds of thousands of tiny, little rules that all combine to make a baby grow into a little person fit for the society they were born into.

You could never consciously absorb it all! It has to be done unconsciously … at least, at first.

There's this famous book called *Rich Dad, Poor Dad*, written by Robert Kiyosaki. He shared in it how, basically, if you come from a poor family, you could struggle your whole life and try to get rich, but you're not going to make it.

And if you come from a rich family, you could be stupid about money your whole life and still make it — not because of how hard you worked or what you did to improve your circumstances, but solely because of the unconscious behavior you downloaded from your rich-minded parents!

So, the rich-minded are making the right moves, whether they know it or not. And the same goes for poor people. They're living by the programs they inherited from their family. Perhaps things like, "you can't make it," "life's a struggle," or "getting rich is hard."

Or even, *"Who do you think you are* to deserve money?"

And if this is anything like the programs you're running on, then for 95% of the day, you *will* sabotage yourself. But only because that's what your program is built for. Poor people stay poor and rich people stay rich because the programming we're running on determines 95% of our life.

And for only 5% of the day can you use your conscious mind to creatively rework those programs.

Quite the uphill battle!

Even though you may think you're just "living your life," your choices and actions are predominantly guided by the programs you've picked up along the way. You just can't see it happen because, like an iceberg, it's occurring under the surface: subconsciously, meaning below the surface.

For 400 years, the Jesuits have been saying, "Give me a child until it's seven years old, and I will show you the man." They were spot on, though nobody believed them because no one understood just how right they were.

They knew that the first seven years serve as the programming period, and how 95% of life lived after that will be determined by whatever the programs are.

In order to observe and shift the programs running your paradigm, you don't have to try and think back to what happened when you were young. You just need to look at your life as it is now.

The things that come into your life easily (good or bad) come in because you have a program to support their survival in your reality. Anything you're struggling with, working hard at, or putting a lot of effort or force into getting must, therefore, not be supported by a program in your subconscious.

Why are you working so hard? You don't need to strong-arm your way through it, the same way you don't have to relive your past. You just need to look at your life now and say to yourself, "Where am I struggling?"

Because wherever it is you find yourself struggling with, there inevitably lies a program in your subconscious mind that does not support your journey to the destination you've been looking for … and while struggling, you've been trying to override the system.

This won't work.

The conscious mind is creative and can learn things in any number of ways. However, the conscious mind cannot reprogram your mindset. The subconscious mind — the one holding all the patterns — just doesn't learn that way.

The subconscious mind naturally learns in one of two fundamental ways: the first being hypnosis, which is how it learns the first seven years of life … But then, after age seven, how do you put new programs in repetition?

The answer is *practice.*

You want to drive a car? You didn't learn by just getting in the seat with a key. You had to practice. Learning the alphabet? How many times did you *go* from A to Z before you knew it?

Eventually, you reach a point where you no longer need to repeat the alphabet, and you've just got it. This happens with anything you do repeatedly.

The subconscious mind can then learn new programs and establish new habits through either **hypnosis** or **repetition.**

I like the latter, as it reminds me of that phrase "fake it till you make it." I'm sure you know it, but if you don't, here's a sample: Let's say you're not a happy person, but you want to be. To become a happy person, repeat to yourself over and over, "I'm happy, I'm happy, I'm happy, I'm happy."

Sure, you may not look happy quite yet. But eventually, your subconscious will listen and catch on. And one day, you'll just turn around and be happy! (Remember, 95% of life comes from the subconscious, so once it clicks, it's in there for good!) And then you won't have to say it to yourself anymore. (Unless you want to!)

It'll be automatic from there on out. Habit formed. Program reformed.

This is why we see people doing affirmations and gratitude journals. If you do that daily, it's repetitive, and eventually, it'll stick!

That's the secret.

Putting a sticky note on the fridge is a reminder, but it isn't repetitive … it's more of a suggestion. Something like this just will not work very well. You have to practice or repeat the action until it becomes a habit.

In this way, you can slowly shift the paradigm shaping your life to one which supports you living your best life!

"The key to success is to focus on goals, not obstacles."

- John Qreshi

THREE

The Nine False Beliefs Keeping You From Success

No matter where you were born, you're no longer living in the same economic environment as the one where you were raised.

I, for one, was brought up with too many programs; too many Myths, which have negatively affected my life by creating obstacles blocking my way to success.

I share with you now nine of the most common Myths about success and money I still see people use today. Absorb the truth to these programs, so you can avoid the mistakes and struggles I've gone through.

False Belief # 1

YOU HAVE TO SAVE TO GET RICH OR GET RICH SLOWLY

We were told, "a penny saved is a penny earned," but I learned the hard way that a penny saved is always a fucking penny. When a recession or bad times come, it's no longer a penny that lasts, but your skill set. If I were to lose everything today, but I still have my skill set, I can make it over and over again to where I want to be in my life. Therefore, it was not saving money, but my skill set that has given me certainty.

Napoleon Hill once said: "If you are in debt and are struggling to pay it off, you do not have a debt problem, you have an *income* problem."

This statement can be applied to this first myth.

What would the level of income have to be for you to — never again — have to worry about saving?

That level where you are bringing in so much capital that you couldn't spend it all, even if you wanted to? Where, now, your money begins to save itself?

That is the level you are aiming for, right?

Well, let me tell you, that level of income is attainable by **anyone who puts in the work** to make it happen.

Attempting to save vast amounts of money means you will have to live on a tight budget, without much room for luxuries.

One of these luxuries is self-investment.

You will likely see more success if you choose to save a smaller amount of money and, instead dedicate the rest to investing in yourself. You could pay for a course or mentorship to learn new skills, or you could use the money for a monetary investment opportunity.

Once you have spent enough on yourself, to the point where you start to see some financial success, your money will begin to save itself … as it accumulates faster than you can spend it.

False Belief # 2

YOU HAVE TO BE PERFECTLY READY

What is 'perfectly ready'?

Let's be honest with ourselves here: A lot of excuses are built on this ideology of being 'ready.'

You may tell yourself you are not ready in many different ways. A lot of us wait for the perfect time or wait for the right thing to happen before we believe we can start. The truth is you will never be ready *until* you start. You have to build a foundation for whatever it is you are trying to do.

Building a framework is perhaps the most important part of any venture, but it's the part that hardly anyone will see. They will see you when you are already successful and not how you started. With this in mind, it becomes clear that you simply need to get started in any way you can.

Having an idea in your head and not acting on it means you have a *dream*. You could have a full list of actions you need to take, all laid out perfectly in a detailed plan, but this still only equates to a dream.

Dreaming that you will one day be successful is simply not enough. You need to have a clear idea of where you want to be and figure out how you are going to get yourself to that point. What you need to focus on is turning your dream into a goal — making your dream attainable.

Now you may ask: How does a dream become a goal? By taking action and tracking your progress.

By taking action and tracking your progress.

You have to be accountable for your actions and have a set path you are following.

A dream is an idea, and a goal is a reality.

So, picture your goal. Think of what it is you desire. Put yourself in that scenario. For you to even have this vision in the first place, you must accept that it is *possible*. People are living this life, and you want to be one of them. It's no fairy tale; it exists, only hard work stands in your way.

There is no such thing as overnight success, but this is what so many of us chase. Whatever your endeavor is, it is critical that you understand that your first step will never be your most successful. But, you have to keep in mind that every step you take is one step closer to that success you desire.

Now, to truly find the path that you need to follow to reach your goal, you need to reverse-engineer your dream. You need to begin with the end goal in mind by picturing where you'd like to be in your ideal world. Now think about where you would have been a month before this vision. And then a month before that. And so on until you get all the way back to the start, where you are now.

If you can figure out what you would have to have done to get to each of these points, you will end up with a reverse plan. Flip this plan around, and you have your beginning-to-end strategy that takes you from where you are now to that dream situation you want.

You have set this plan yourself; it's not been set by anyone else, so you have no reason not to follow it. Yes, you can tweak it along the way, but you should maintain the core values throughout your journey.

False Belief # 3

YOU ARE NOT BUSINESS-MINDED AND THEREFORE YOU CAN'T BE RICH

To put this myth to rest, there is one fact you must become aware of: Business is a skill that can be taught and learned.

Being 'business minded' is a skill that not one person on the planet was born with. No infant or child understands the core principles of business. By their teenage years, most adolescents have not even started to grasp this concept. It is only in adult life that most of us start to become interested in the world of business.

Why?

It is quite simple: Business requires a mature mindset and an understanding of the core values of a human. It is very unlikely you will make a good businessperson if you don't know what makes a person tick. The whole industry, in its simplest form, revolves around buying and selling.

Of course, when you dig deeper, there are more forms of 'business,' but when you strip them all back, they all come back to someone buying something, and therefore someone selling something.

To confirm this, let's take a look at the definition of the term 'business': "An organization or economic system where goods and services are exchanged for one another or for money."

False Belief # 4

YOU HAVE TO GO TO COLLEGE, FIND A JOB AND WORK HARD UNTIL YOU FIND LUCK

There are many advocates of the theory that the modem schooling system is broken and, in some cases, irrelevant in today's economy. I happen to be one of them. Employers often look for experience over qualification, and therefore, students find themselves in unprecedented amounts of debt after graduating to then find themselves with no real career prospects.

A qualification can only get you so far, and it comes with the stigma of being 'theory-based.' And in today's world, that means it is essentially useless.

However, many of us fall into the trap of believing that you cannot get anywhere near your goals without a relevant degree. If you did not go to college or university, it is by no means too late for you! You have to remember, a lot of the most successful people in the world had no schooling past high school.

Take Bill Gates, for example. Once the richest man in the world, not many know he dropped out of Harvard in 1975 to found Microsoft. Just a year later, Steve Jobs left college to backpack through India. He then went on to build Apple and passed away in 2011 with a net worth of approximately 11 billion dollars. Facebook founder Mark Zuckerberg is another Harvard dropout. He left the prestigious university in 2005, and as of 2016, Facebook is worth more than 200 billion dollars.

What do all of these men have in common? They believed in themselves to the extent that they would walk away from the highest level of educational certification in order to pursue their personal goals.

Now, it is important to realize these cases happened in the past. As a race, we are now in our technological prime, and the Internet has never offered us more. There are many resources available online for gaining knowledge and experience in your chosen field. You could find a mentor online, take a course, or simply browse articles and the like.

Needless to say, whatever field you choose to apply yourself within, there is information available to you. You just have to take it.

Do you really want to work for an employer? Have you had a job you hated before? Do you like trading your valuable time for the small amount you are paid?

The answer to all three of these questions is no, of course.

So why do we sentence ourselves to a life working within a company that doesn't care about us? Why do we chase promotions in a job we do not even enjoy? Will the money make it more bearable?

That's the question we all need to get the truthful answer to.

If someone offered you a million dollars a year to do a job you hate, would you take it?

Think about it for a minute. Play out the situation in your head.

I want you to imagine you working that job you hate.

For a lot of us, it means sitting in an office with a stack of papers in front of us, working towards an impossible deadline set by our boss, hopped up on caffeine as a result of all that coffee you chug down during the day to keep yourself going.

For others, it means working in retail, dealing with another angry customer, settling them down over an issue that had nothing to do with you, promising them that everything will be better for them next time.

Maybe you've completed some downright derogatory tasks in your past. Maybe when you think of work, you think of cleaning toilets, scrubbing floors, or running random errands all to benefit someone else's sheer laziness.

Does any of this sound familiar? Can you relate any of your past work experience to these types of situations?

If you can, then you can use this to your advantage. These experiences are strengths and not weaknesses.

How?

Well, every time you consider giving up on what you really want, all to take the 'easy' path of just working for an employer for the rest of your days, I want you to remember these times. Every time you think to yourself: "It wasn't that bad. I could be happy just taking orders from someone else," I want you to mentally slap yourself in the face.

It is *that bad.* You will never be happy this way. Accept it, and start working towards what you *actually* want.

Now, if you have never experienced any of the feelings or situations I talked about above, if you have never felt tired, degraded, or under intense pressure from any of your workplaces, then consider yourself lucky. But you don't ever want to find yourself there, so you should also take the same steps in working towards your goal. Allow your motivation to be that you never want to see how bad it *can* get.

Having a demanding boss can really get in your head and make for some mental health issues you never thought would come from work. Bad bosses can make you feel worthless if they want. They can watch you do a job to your highest ability and then tell you it's not good enough. They will send you messages or emails on your day off telling you that yesterday's work wasn't good enough.

Don't get me wrong; there are good employers out there who won't treat you this way. If you find one of these, consider yourself lucky. Most bosses have some element of negative leadership style within them because this is how they were trained by their boss.

It is like a circle; your negative boss was trained to be that way by his negative boss, and his boss also trained him that way and so on. To find a 'good' employer in this day and age, you would have to discover someone who has chosen to break the mold and make a conscious decision to be a positive influence on their employees' lives.

When you are at work 40–50 hours of the week, you have to commute to your workplace, you leave early and get home late, and when you do finally arrive home, you are physically and mentally drained from the work you've done that day.

When you get stuck in this cycle, you can watch days and weeks go by with little to no progress on your plan. For example, if you work a full-time job from Monday to Friday, it's very easy to put everything on hold during the week and try to work on yourself and your goals only on the weekends. But you have to admit to yourself that this is not going to work.

Two days of the seven-day week is not enough to make a real impact on your life. If you are spending these entire two days improving yourself and completing your personal development tasks, then you are not including any leisure time for yourself, which can be detrimental to results.

You need to remember to give yourself time off so that you do not experience burnout, which can cause you to lose motivation and deplete your overall energy levels.

The best thing you can do to avoid all of the negative outcomes I have discussed within this section is to create a detailed schedule of your ideal week and *stick to it.*

Write down when you are scheduled to be working, and leave an hour either side of your shifts to allow for travel and work preparation. Write down when you'd like to work on self-development work and remember to include leisure time. It is also very important to ensure you are getting eight hours of quality sleep every night, so you are rested and refreshed for the next day.

Sticking to your own schedule requires a particular discipline that most people do not possess.

Picture this situation: You wake up on a Saturday morning. Your alarm goes off at 7am, and you know you *have* to get out of bed right away. Most people would see pressing snooze and sleeping for another hour or two as not a big deal, but if you do this, you are putting your entire day on hold for that hour or two, which means you won't finish on time. That means you'll go to bed later tonight, and then inevitably, you will wake up later tomorrow. It's a vicious cycle you cannot afford to get trapped in.

False Belief # 5

I DON'T KNOW ANY RICH PEOPLE. THEREFORE I CAN'T BE RICH

We have all heard the saying that you are the average of the people you spend the most time with. There are studies that show that elements of this saying hold true. However, when you look at it from a financial perspective, you need to have a different view.

Just because you may not know or socialize with any rich people does not ban you from becoming one.

It would be almost ridiculous to assume that just because you have no affiliation with wealthy people you cannot become one of them. Wealthy people simply find it easier to make money because, for the most part, they have access to more money than you do.

Remember, wealth creates wealth, and some people just have a better starting point than others. Think, if someone receives ten thousand dollars for their inheritance at eighteen years old, and their parents are financial advisors, do you think that person has a good chance of becoming rich off that ten grand?

Of course they do. They just had a better foundation built for them. However, to think you cannot create your own foundation later on in life is ludicrous.

Wealth creates more wealth. If you have a small amount of money, it's difficult to find opportunity.

If one is to master the skill set, he/she can create anything on this planet by offering the right strategy to the right people at the right time.

False Belief # 6

YOU HAVE TO BE LUCKY TO BE SUCCESSFUL

Hope and Luck are the two dangerous things you can rely on, rather than relying on your actions.

Luck: the mythical entity that follows us all, but can never be proven to even exist.

We wish it to others, we wish it upon ourselves, and we blame it when things go wrong.

Are you really going to rely on it?

I will tell you right now, luck cannot and should not EVER be relied on for success.

That is not to say that good things cannot happen by chance and are therefore attributed as 'lucky.' But, you can never count on it if these situations occur. To take this a step further, let's take a look at the definition of the word 'luck.'

'Luck' is the "success or failure apparently brought by chance rather than through one's own actions."

I think we can all agree that this is an accurate representation of what luck is. So if this is what luck really is, then we can all agree it's not a useful tool for us unless it makes itself so.

We cannot employ it or control it in any way; good luck and bad luck comes to us in whichever way it pleases. So it is better for us to simply ignore it as a factor.

Like many things, luck is simply a social construct thought up by humans many, many years ago. It doesn't physically exist, so that means that, in essence, it is just an idea that someone came up with, and it caught on. It's like any other spiritual belief, like karma or the Law of Attraction.

Just because these ideas exist and are discussed frequently by people doesn't mean they even necessarily exist or have any bearing on your personal success, so it makes more sense for you to simply ignore them all.

False Belief # 7

YOU HAVE TO WIN A LOTTERY

This myth is related very closely to the previous one. To win a lottery you have to rely on luck. If you read the last section, you'll know that this is not a viable option for you if you are trying to work towards your goal.

When you're hoping to win the lottery, you may be conditioning your mind the idea that, "I am too dumb to do anything, and my only option for survival is to win a lottery."

Taking note of past lottery winners, most of whom have either gone bankrupt or died.

Jim Rohn has said that if you distribute the wealth of the richest people equally to all the seven billion people in the world, it will soon come back to all the pockets from where it originated: those original rich folks.

You see, it's all about the mindset one needs on how to accumulate wealth, how to keep money, how to invest money, and how to multiply it. You cannot do that by hoping to win a lottery.

Just imagine you spend your whole life waiting to win a lottery to fund all of your ideas to make your goal a reality, and you never win. You die unhappy and unfulfilled.

Now, I don't mean to be morbid, but this is the type of reality you have to believe will happen if you want to fast-track your own success. You cannot afford to even consider taking the chance of waiting for a lottery win to start making moves.

Perhaps you are stalling, chasing your goals because you believe if you win the lottery, you will never have to make the effort to work towards it.

Well, you can look at many successful entrepreneurs and they will all tell you the journey is the most enjoyable part of the victory.

Winning a lottery to skip to the end is essentially cheating, and it means you will miss out on the best part: the journey itself.

Not to mention that the chances of actually winning the lottery are insanely low and every ticket you buy means you have less money to spend on real opportunities for yourself.

False Belief # 8

YOU HAVE TO WORK VERY HARD TO MAKE MONEY

In the last few years, an argument has been brought to light by several successful entrepreneurs:

Money is nothing more than the by-Product of value creation.

It's not just about working hard, but about moving outside of your comfort zone every day, mastering the right skill set, and delivering a valuable outcome to the market's needs.

It's not as necessary to work hard as it is to provide value to the marketplace.

Money is simply an exchange for the value you are providing.

If you ask most people how to make more money, they will tell you to work harder, get a second job, get another shift, or work overtime. I call this the hustling approach: You hope and pray that it's all going to work out one day, and you basically try it all, spreading your time and energy to do your best, and yet, the results are very weak.

Instead of working more hours, what if you increased the value of your hours? What if you improved your skills and delivered more value?

This argument has thrown the entire philosophy of working hard to earn money into the trash. The problem is that the generation above ours — some of the most influential people in our lives (our parents) — were raised on this philosophy. To suggest to them that a high income can be earned without having to work hard for it is ludicrous to them. They don't believe it to be possible, and therefore, they try to steer us away from believing it as well.

They do so with the best of intentions. They don't want to see us fail in life, so they believe that if we just do as they did and work hard for our pay, then we might just be alright.

What they don't take into consideration is how much times have changed. Particularly in terms of technology and the Internet, it is indeed possible to make a considerable income without having to work for an employer.

This 'digital nomad' lifestyle is, of course, frowned upon by our elders, and so it creates a rift between us. This can sometimes be enough of a reason in itself to give up on our dreams. We don't want to fail and disappoint our parents, or even worse, prove them right by failing, so you choose to never even try in the first place.

This is one of the saddest scenarios I hear about, and I urge all people who bring this to my attention to grasp hold of their *own* lives and their *own* goals and take charge.

And it is your job to recognize where those opportunities are.

You will probably not be able to get to your end goal by only using one or the other; you will have to work smart, work hard, and sometimes do both at the same time.

False Belief # 9

MONEY CAN'T BUY YOU HAPPINESS!

Money can't buy happiness, but a lack of money is the passport to Misery.

It complicates life so much that money has become an important problem to be solved.

If someone says that money is not important and that they can live on love, well then I say, "Go to a bank and deposit the love to pay the rent."

Money matters for so many things: food, shelter, medicine. You've got to have money to facilitate the important things.

My parents have always told me not to touch money and I grew up with a phrase that 'money is the root of all evil and will not make you happy.'

Well guess what?!

In my early twenties, I was broke with an eviction notice from my landlord. Money was everything for me to survive my life.

Money can buy you anything you want it to. Create your happiness, and then buy it, simple. And of course, it can get you an Uber ride.

Think about your dream reality, and how much it would cost in total.

Consider all the material objects you'd like to have, and how much you'd be spending monthly on assets such as your house or your car.

This would all cost a lot of money, right?

Would you be happy if you had all these things and you could comfortably afford it? Well then, point proven. Money *can* buy you happiness. You just have to apply it in the correct way.

As do you have to apply *the truth* of each of these nine myths to your everyday life in the correct way. Once you can pierce through the veils of illusion that these myths have created in your life, you can also observe where else in your life you are living in limitation. Limitations that others created, no less.

You are free to create your own rules and live by them. The work comes in showing up to see your patterns, to see the myths in your mind, and to then support your changing concepts with changed *action.*

"Being aware of your fear is smart. Overcoming it is the mark of a successful person."

- Seth Godin

FOUR

The Power Of Emptying The Cup

Writing something down can help you to release your attachment to it. Most of us are aware of or have experienced this at some point in our lives. However, when I became a master trainer in Neuro-Linguistic Programming, neuroscience, and quantum physics, I realized that there was more to it.

When you physically write something down, you open up your neurology. When you *take the time* to go and get a pen, find some paper, and expend the physical and mental effort to actually write it down, you are more likely to learn something from it. When you make this conscious effort to complete the task of writing, the effect is more effective!

I learned this from my mentor Dr. Hew Len, and since I have applied this principle, it has changed my life. "If you do these five things every day, you will become the greatest leader on the planet: Every day you read, every day you write, every day you learn, every day you unlearn and every day, you re-learn."

Well, this is the basis of "emptying the cup." An activity designed to help you get all the bad feelings out, so that they no longer affect you. Emptying the cup is like a detox; you are emptying your filled-up brain (your cup) of all the neurologically-bound bad habits and thoughts you possess.

By writing down the bad thoughts and feelings, you are opening up your neurology and your neural network pathways. This is part of the process of Neuroplasticity, one of the proven ways of reprogramming your unconscious mind.

Now, go get a pen. Grab a piece of paper and tell this piece of paper how you feel. Write down all — and I mean ALL — the crap in your head. All the things in your life that you just cannot stand!

Complain about your life and then ask yourself, "What do I have to learn from this?"

Now, write down all the negative words that could be used to describe you, words you no longer want to be associated with.

Write until you physically, mentally, and emotionally cannot think of another negative thing to do with your life that you haven't already written.

Then, the task is complete.

You can now take a look at your results. Read your page(s) through a couple of times to make sure all is complete. Add anything else you can think of until you're pretty sure you're empty.

You have just emptied your cup! Now you can begin to adopt new life habits, new goals, and a new mindset.

But, most importantly, you can now ask yourself, "What do *I really* want?!?"

Think of the lifestyle you will lead when you reach your goal. Think of what your house will look like, what cars you will have, how your family will live, and all the other parts of your dream life you will be able to enjoy.

This is what you need to fill your cup with. Fill it up with these ambitions. Become driven by them.

You have now, 1) emptied your cup, 2) established what can be learned from the pain, and 3) filled it with the good.

You are ready to move forward and take the first steps towards your goals. You have permission to enter the big, bad world now.

In completing this exercise, you can now look at things with fresh vision, a vision aligned with your goals. You will see things differently and absorb information in a new way. You may carry yourself differently than before; you may feel more confident. You might feel more ambitious than you previously did, or perhaps more invigorated, like the old flame just had fuel thrown over it.

Feels good, doesn't it?

"I think it is possible for ordinary people to choose to be extraordinary."

- Elon Musk

FIVE

Breaking And Rebuilding Your New Identity

There are invisible forces all around us, and they control everything in our life, including our basic needs. The one most powerful force that directs you virtually every second of your life is the power of emotion.

Change your emotions, and you can change your life.

Your emotion comes from the beliefs you hold, your beliefs come from the story you are telling yourself, and your story comes from the stimulus and your environment. This builds your identity.

Thus, your beliefs affect your reality.

While I was studying to become a Master Trainer in Neuro-Linguistic Programming, a fellow board member and I were researching and discovered that your beliefs determine the reality that you perceive.

In other words:

1. Your beliefs determine your perception of reality.

2. You then, immediately, automatically, (and usually unconsciously) interpret your perception of reality. That is, you (arbitrarily) assign, project, and "superimpose" an interpretation onto your perception of reality.

3. You then emotionally react to your interpretation of that reality.

4. You then have thoughts about this reality.

5. Then, based on your emotions and thoughts, you take action.

Now, you understand that **the story you have been telling yourself** and **the programs in your unconscious mind** are controlling you. You understand **the myths we were all told are untrue.** And you now understand how to **empty your cup** so you can install new programs.

Now, **it's time to break free from myths.**

If you search through Merriam-Webster's dictionary, you will find one word matching one meaning …maybe two or three variations of similar meaning. In school, we were taught to learn only through linear thinking, which limits your neural network pathways to think more broadly.

However, I have learned through the study of quantum physics that in order to open the neurology of your mind and those neural network pathways, you have to think laterally.

And how do you think laterally?

By understanding that everything in this world is a paradox. Nothing is black and white.

We are but human, but we are also the co-creators of our lives. And we can be either creative or destructive in how we craft our lives.

The subconscious mind works day and night. When you begin to use it properly, to your own advantage, your entire life will change for the better.

Think on this for a moment: All that's required to put the science of getting rich to work in your life is a decision.

Most people will look at that and say, "There's got to be more to it than that!"

But how many of you have been trying to earn a lot of money for quite a long time? And how many have difficulty? You know, 1% of the population earns about 96% of all the money that's being earned, and it's a subject that is not taught in school.

When someone comes along and tells you that all you have to do to have what you want is to make a decision, we have a difficult time buying into it. Most likely, because we've worked fairly hard attempting to earn money, and it's hard to even imagine that all that hard work could've been for nothing. That it could even be so simple!

I fell upon this information about three years ago, and I've been absolutely fascinated with it ever since. It takes up all my days. All my time. Somebody could ask me, "What are your hobbies?" And honestly, they're comprised just of studying this subject. It's all I do.

I have worked all over the world with this, and it doesn't really matter where you go. You can go into different countries, into different cultures, but once you get past the culture, people are essentially the same. And I think we all want pretty much the same things.

Back in 2008, I was sharing in conversation with this man when he started drawing a large "R" on this sheet of paper. Then, he put three letters down beside it, and he said that it represents happiness, health, and wealth. And then he asked me if I thought he was a happy guy.

I said, "Yeah." He seemed pretty happy to me.

He asked, "Have you ever seen me when I was sick?" And I had to admit that I hadn't.

He asked, "Have you ever seen me when I was broke?" And again, I had to admit I hadn't.

"Well," he said to me, "you've got to be one of the most miserable people that I have ever met."

And I was. I was an unhappy guy.

I was young, but as I look back at it, I think I was just an unhappy kid who grew up and just stayed that way. And I believe a lot of people live that way; there's a lot of unhappy people around.

I didn't have a terminal illness, but I always had a cold or a headache or a backache or *something* wrong to complain about. And when it came to money, I definitely had a problem.

As this man carried on, he said to me, "You're striking out in all of these areas."

I was actually earning $4,000 a year at the time, and I owed six. Now, you and I both know that that's not an uncommon position for a person to be in. If I took everything I earned in 18 months, left nothing to live on, and only paid my debts, I would have just broken even. Hopefully. So when you look at that, you know there's not a lot of hope.

I don't think I ever thought I'd get out of debt. Not *really*. It never even entered my mind that I *could*. I never considered earning a lot of money, and anyway, I was too busy just trying to keep the wolf away from the door to have done so.

You know, the phone would ring every day with the question, "Where's the money?" And hell, I thought, *If I knew where the money was, you wouldn't have to phone me!*

If you've been there, I get this. I *feel* this. This was a constant problem for me.

I have often said that you'll be absolutely amazed at how much free time you have when you never have to think about money again. Do you know that people spend an enormous amount of time thinking about money if they haven't got it?

Now, if they have got it, it's a totally different story. Just think of the freedom! The mind capacity to spend on other things!

Wallace Wattles wrote a book on the science of getting rich way back in 1903. He said, "You don't get rich by doing certain things. You get rich by doing things in a certain way.

As soon as I read this, I thought, "Yes!! You could totally find two people doing the exact same thing without being able to tell the difference, but still, one is doing it in a certain way and the other isn't."

Thus, their results will be different.

You see, it has to do with intent. It has to do with the energy you're doing things with.

So, to break free from the myths of your life, all you need to do is witness the pattern as it's been and *consciously choose again.* Make a new choice, and don't be afraid to make the choice again and again until you know what's right for you.

Be intentional with your decisions to take advantage of the fact that we are the co-creators of our lives!

"To succeed in life, you need two things: ignorance and confidence"

- Mark Twain

SIX

The Six Levels Of Transformation

I've recognized six key aspects that combine to create true transformation in your life.

ENVIRONMENT

Your environment is more important than your willpower.

If your environment is not supporting your growth, then no matter how hard you try, things won't go as you desire. I remember when I was young, living in my communist homeland and around bad friends and limiting beliefs, I was struggling, I was hustling, and I was broke.

Truth was, I was in a bad environment — bad, meaning, not conducive to growth, an environment that wasn't helping me get where I wanted to go.

I have a lot of determination and drive to succeed, but I was not succeeding because of the environment I was surrounded by.

Your environment has also to do with your focus and the level of commitment of people around you. Their momentum will undoubtedly affect your own. Like my mentor said, "Show me your friends, and I will show you your future."

BEHAVIOR

If you do the same thing over and over, you will keep getting the same results.

It's quite a cliché to say that how you do one *thing* is how you do *everything,* but it proves true. Behavior is rooted in your beliefs. In other words, your belief gives you your identity; it builds the basis for who you are.

Choose with precision, rather than passiveness or cynicism. What you do matters to the person you wish to become, because this is a key to success: Successful people are very intentional about their beliefs and their behaviors.

CAPABILITIES OR HABITS

Habits are something we create from our programs.

When I was researching the human mind and behavior with one of my fellow neuroscientists, we discovered that it's not about the habits we give up on. Some habits stay with us, and it's hard to quit them because they are programmed into our unconscious mind.

In another sense, they are integrated into you, so when changing a habit, it's not just about performing the habits but integrating them. It's not about discipline; it's about integrating the habit into your mind — inside of you — so that it becomes a program in your unconscious mind.

BELIEF

Believe it's possible; believe you have time to do it.

Believing in your dream is the most crucial part of making it happen, and it can take your entire life if you don't give up the bullshit beliefs you've been feeding yourself.

Your belief either limits you or expands you, depending upon what beliefs you are giving yourself. We all were born dumb, naked, and speechless, remember, but later on, as we grew up, we learned and grew into certain beliefs about ourselves. And through our failures, we've given ourselves bullshit beliefs that we are not good enough, or we are not capable enough.

Belief is the only thing where, if one gets it right, it gives them a **powerful** identity shift.

VALUES

If you don't value growth learning, then how will you engage with the world around you?

What values are you following? Do you hold the value of believing money is the root of all evil? Do you hold the value of believing life is all about *eat, sleep, and repeat,* or the value that life isn't fair?

Or do you hold values of an entrepreneurial mindset that follows problems up with questions, such as, "How can I do that, how can I afford it, how can I succeed, what do I need to do, what works, what doesn't work, or what am I doing now?"

When you get your values right, you open your mind and rewire your brain. In other words: A question opens the mind and a statement closes the mind.

IDENTITY

I am a procrastinator. I am strong. I am …

Belief gives you your identity, and your identity is the only thing that surrounds and determines your present and future. It sounds so simple, but it's very deep, and complex and it comes back to "What is the story you are telling yourself?"

What limiting beliefs are you giving to yourself?

To maximize your efforts toward success, all six of these aspects have to be aligned. Then, and only then, true transformation can take place.

"If you want to change the world, first you must change yourself."

-Anonymous

SEVEN

The Deepest And Most Hidden Layer Of All Belief: "I Am Not Good Enough"

The biggest power inside the human mind is one's self-image (i.e., what image they are giving themselves).

I have learned this from my *mentor Dr. Adriana James*/. *Your life reflects upon what self-image you're giving yourself.*

When I was in my late teens to mid-twenties, even though I'd experienced so many failures and setbacks, once I found that I'd learned something new, or figured something out, I became instantly entitled! I became a know-it-all and acted the part very well.

Once I entered into the world of neuroscience and quantum physics, however, I grew obsessed with these fields, and realized just how little I knew … and thus, was in a perpetual state of seeking to learn!

After a decade of research, I've realized that I now know something unequivocally useful and important, yes, but that there is always more. The evolution, the innovation is intrepid.

Before I started writing this book, I was looking for the Magic Pill that would finally make me feel like I Am Good Enough. Now, I've found the Magic Pill! I truly have! And as soon as I found it, I felt amazing for the first time in my entire life.

But what I didn't expect was to uncover that the Magic Pill I was looking for was *actually inside of me all along.*

You see, there are two different kinds of Confident. Two different kinds of Self-Worth. The first is arrogance, where a person will fake it till they make it. The problem with this is that deep inside, all those programs, all those insecurities, are still running. They don't stop just because they're ignored.

This kind of confidence only faces the demons inside from time to time, which just doesn't solve the problem.

The power of true **I Am Good Enough** comes when a person understands that they are enough just as they are. *These are* my *skills, and these are* my *weaknesses, and I accept them both. I am who I am.* Finding yourself out and accepting yourself — strengths *and* weaknesses — is what makes you good enough.

It's a long journey. I'm not gonna lie. Possibly, it'll take you your whole life just to find out who you are. But — and here's the kicker — once you find out, and resolve the inner world inside of you, the questions lingering in the outside world resolve all by themselves. Like magic, but so, so *real.* One by one, they vanish, along with the illusions you once bought into.

There is a cliché quote that says that "all answers are inside of you," and really, it's very true.

It all comes down to mastering your unconscious mind. Which, as it happens, is ignored by 99% of the people on this planet. But *how* can we ignore 99% of who we are? The key is to use your unconscious mind 'consciously,' as opposed to 'by default' — which is the pitfall many fall into.

The unconscious mind is the intermediary through which one may draw upon the forces of Infinite Intelligence at will. It contains the secret process by which mental impulses are modified into their spiritual equivalent. It is, in fact, the medium through which focused thought and intention may be forged into reality.

And it is the seat of our power. When we can tap into the power of our mind, and use it for good, we tap into our own empowerment. Suddenly, it isn't such a big problem, our feeling bad about ourselves. Suddenly, it's easy to see our own worth. For you to see that, truly, **I Am Good Enough.**

PART TWO

"If your mind was free, who'll you seek to transform the planet"

- Dr. Adriana James

EIGHT

Your Three Superpowers

Reading this chapter's title, you might be wondering, "What could my three superpowers be?"

"Is it my writing? My business? Is it a talent that I may not have discovered yet?"

They're none of these things. But your superpowers are more potent than any of those. They're the reason entrepreneurs, writers, artists, actors, and great athletes are phenomenal. They're the catalyst for successful businesspeople all across the globe.

In fact, there are three superpowers every single human being is born with. These three powers are the engines that run every other skill set, talent, or passion you possess.

These superpowers are built inside of you, and when you can access them, you can then build other superpowers upon them within the wells of your reservoir.

These **three superpowers** are:

1. The Power of Your Goals
2. The Power of Your Story
3. The Power of Your Why

1. The Power of Your Goals

You see, your unconscious mind is very powerful. And when you begin to set your goals, you start signaling new thoughts to your unconscious mind. Then these thoughts can become your new identity, setting the course for your life and for your future.

So, if you want to fix your future, fix your identity. And *how* can you do this?

By setting clear goals. Meaning, when you say to yourself, deep inside, "I am shitty," guess what will happen? Your day is going to be shitty, and you will feel shitty about yourself and your life.

However, when you say to yourself deep inside, something like, "Life loves me," you will feel and focus your attention on all the ways in which your life does indeed love you!

Now, this is not simply in line with the Law of Attraction, but it is a large chunk of what Napoleon Hill shares as the Laws of the Universe.

This is deep, subconscious work, but when you can **set clear goals** for how you want to feel about your life and yourself, you can shift these programs. This will then allow you to shift your identity and shift your life.

2. The Power of Your Story

We all have a story. However, some stories are weaker than others. Our story is our identity, and when you have a positive sense of self, you build a compelling story. We all love to hear stories of "doers" who change the world — people with the belief in themselves necessary to accomplish great things.

We all have that Hero/Heroine inside of us. Every single person reading this text can achieve greatness. To experience true excellence, though, you need to see this person for yourself. You need to envision your success and crystalize it.

If you don't believe in yourself, how can you expect others to believe in you? Put another way, how will you achieve success on a grand scale unless you think you have the capacity to make it?

Successful entrepreneurs, athletes, and other skilled figures dedicate immense time, energy, and resources to be successful. Wayne Gretzky did not step on the hockey rink for the first time knowing how to score hundreds of goals. He stepped on the ice fumbling and stumbling, just like the first time anyone else skates.

He was immensely successful. He committed to becoming an incredibly excellent hockey player and took massive action to ensure that it happened. That commitment started at the beginning of his life.

It started with a mental story he was composing for himself. It began with a dream and a vision.

Our story can either propel us or bog us down. Our stories can make us achieve great things and accomplish new feats like Gretzky, or it can provide us a perpetual belief that "I can't do anything." Sadly, far too many people choose the latter. If you're reading this, though, know that you can choose greatness. It's within you. You just need to defeat the negativity that surrounds you and lives within you.

Many people struggle with a positive self-image. They fill their minds with constant doubt and worry. They see somebody like Gretzky skating, and instead of thinking to themselves, "Wow, how can I learn to skate like that?" they think, "Ugh, I'll never be that good." These voices act like villains in their heads. These villains are belittling and condescending. They convince you that not only are you not good enough now but that you will never be good enough in the future.

Great guitarists were not born with the ability to play songs immediately. All guitarists will talk about the work — the story, the journey — that it took to develop their skills. The difference between the great players and those that buy a guitar, play for a bit, and never try again is that the great ones believed they could succeed. They saw the guitar as the beginning of their story, not a small aside.

The villain voices in your head and around you are wrong. They seek control by trying to lock your potential. If you don't believe you can, then you'll never attempt anything. If you never try, you'll "succeed" 100% of the time.

To fight these beliefs, you must remember the other character as well. Every great story has both a villain and a hero. You are the hero. You are the central figure in your life — the one that perseveres, conquers, and achieves a great victory. If you work to nurture your inner hero, then it can take over by changing "I'll never be able to do that" to "Of course I can do that, let's figure out how."

That is a game-changing mentality that unlocks potential. For example, you can make $1 million a year. Countless people all over the world are doing that right now. What is the story — your story — that will allow you to accomplish that goal? There is a solution to this problem, and your inner hero wholeheartedly believes that it exists. Let it figure out the right way to accomplish your dreams!

Note that you do not need to become someone you aren't to be successful. The story concept is not about adopting someone else's journey and mimicking it. Remember that the superpower we're discussing is "the power of your story." No matter if you're an introvert, an extrovert, highly intelligent, or of average intelligence, there is a path forward to achieve your dreams.

Your story is unique. It will leverage your strengths to create resounding success for all your goals. Your life events won't mirror other successful people, but you have to be 100% committed that your unique life circumstances, skills, and ability to acquire new talents will end up the way you envision.

You should have full confidence in yourself. Many issues arise by having low confidence — not zero confidence — but having a confidence drop, that's enough to cause pause. It's enough of a drop to make you doubt yourself just a bit. The confidence drop makes you question your story and doubt the ending that you have envisioned for yourself. Having 100% confidence in yourself, in your visions and your dreams, leaves no space for the evil voices in your head and coming from those around you to take over.

Every person who has ever learned new skills knows about "plateauing." When you acquire a unique ability, there comes a point in time when you seemingly cannot get better. You can only skate so fast, or you can only throw a baseball so quickly. If your confidence is not 100% but 95%, you might have doubts. You might think, "Maybe this is it; maybe this is as good as I will ever be." Unfortunately, that turns into a self-fulfilling prophecy.

Instead, keep your confidence at 100%. Always remember that your unique story is not over yet. There are still many chapters and sentences to write. More importantly, the ending you see is within reach. Keep growing, keep aspiring, and you'll be able to unlock the incredible potential of your unique life story!

3. The Power of Your Why

So many people get lost in their passions. And when they can't find or figure out their passion, they end up feeling lost, or just don't know what to do.

You can't succeed in something long term until you discover "Why" you want to do it.

It's not necessary for you to figure out your passion *if* you can instead focus on figuring out your *Why*. Your *Why* is the reason you get up in the morning; it serves as the main motivating force behind all of your actions.

With your *Why*, when you want to do something, you will initiate a powerful signal in your neurology to make *this* your purpose, where then it becomes your motivator.

Just as Apple got advice from Simon Sinek, when I first moved to New York City and was looking for a mentor, I found Daymond John from Shark Tank. I got the chance to meet him at a conference, wherein I acquired the opportunity to learn from the most inspiring investor, business consultant, and entrepreneur. I started taking mentorship lessons from Daymond John, and the very first thing he taught me was to find my *Why*.

Today, Apple has their *Why* because of Simon Sinek. And the **moment** they found theirs, Apple went from not even being on the map to becoming one of the top four fortune 500 companies in the world.

When I found my *Why*, it ignited a spark that lit up all the dark in my life.

So before you start anything, find your *Why*. *Why* do you want to do what you do? What does it do for you? Once you find your *Why*, then your *What* and *How* will reveal themselves gracefully.

You see, a lot of people fail in their life and business because they look for their *How* or their *What* before they know their *Why*. And when you don't have your *Why*, it's like you are sailing on a boat without a purpose.

Sure, the view is nice, but where are you going? And more importantly, *Why?!?*

When you don't have a purpose, no matter how great and lucrative your business plan, sooner or later, you will hit challenges. And your mindset will not able to handle it, and you are sure to either give up or transition to another business.

Purpose up. Find your *Why*, and let it inform all that you do and how you do it.

You can't succeed in something long term until you discover "Why" you want to do it.

"We never lack people with money. We lack people with dreams, who can die for those dreams."

- Jack Ma

NINE

The 20 Secrets Of Successful People

I have experienced a financial crash firsthand, I've gone through many big failures, and I've had people stab me in the back. But it's okay — it's all okay — because I choose to grow from it!

I choose to get stronger, and I choose to believe in myself, knowing I can do more when I stand in that belief.

That's spirituality, you know?

People who are afraid of making mistakes — what they teach in school and program into your mind — don't grow, because, in spirituality, everything is a paradox.

Entwined in every failure is some success and with every triumph, there is failure still to learn from.

There is good, and there is bad. There is right, and there is wrong. There is up, and there is down. It all exists, and it's all good. It's all going to be okay, and it'll be even better when you can choose to grow from it!

Most people want to be always right, but unfortunately, you can't have that. It isn't reality and for the average person, the reason they are poor is because they have not failed enough.

You're not in school anymore. Now you get to decide who you want to be. How you want to show up.

You get to redefine what safety is *to you.*

When you decide to become successful, you want to create a machine that can monetize. You want to make a lot of money so you can give it away and you can't do that when you are broke.

So let's take a look into the 20 Secrets of Successful People!

1 . GET COMFORTABLE BEING UNCOMFORTABLE!

Your comfort zone is your income zone.

I've studied the richest and most successful people on this planet and they all have one thing in common: They never stay in their comfort zone for very long. They are constantly moving. And I see many people become inactive out of the fear of being judged, but people like almost anything when it comes in its purest form.

In other words, when your intent is right, people are going to love you.

Humans are naturally inclined to dislike change. It's just the way we are programmed.

We get comfortable with our surroundings. We get comfortable with our friends, our jobs, and our nice routines, and we choose not to test the waters with anything new as it might not work as well.

We don't want to have to go to the effort of learning anything new, as we already know a way to do it. It's natural.

But to be a true innovator, you need to be ready to embrace change. You need to be the one who is willing to step way outside the box and think creatively.

And don't fear the judgments!

People will accept anyone and anything, so long as they authentically show up as who they truly are. So just be yourself. People are stunningly accepting of anything they actually believe is pure in form.

Just be you. When your intentions are pure, people will notice the difference. When you are trying to fake or force something, and have an inauthentic intent, then that's a disaster. That's when you come to experience the "hate."

I know what my intent is, so what do I have to be scared of? Can other people's hate really take anything away from me? Or can I know my strength, and know what I am capable of overcoming?

Say I want to build the biggest building in town, and how I want to do that is simply by doing it, by building the biggest building in town, but most people want to build a building by tearing down everyone else who is building around them, so they alone can stand out.

2. MONEY LOVES SPEED!

Wealth is measured more* in time *than money.

If someone earns 25k per month, after forty years of earning the same amount, they have earned a million dollars in total; on the other hand, someone who has made a million dollars in one year has made a huge difference in their life.

The value you provide X how many people you serve = your money.

When most people consider the idea of becoming rich quickly, they think it's not possible, or they think it must be something shady.

Wealth is measured in the amount of time you are able to produce, and the only way you can do this is by delivering a valuable outcome to the marketplace. I will talk more about this in point #9. But there is one more thing you need to have other than speed, which is Commitment.

Every time I've been able to commit to an action without doubt in my decision, I've ended up without any regrets in the end.

You see, we always get stretched when we learn. And committing first, deciding later, has been my number one formula for going all in. Like Tony Robbins said, "There is no failure, there is only feedback."

I understand it this way: Why overthink if you have committed to doing something? The action alone is the commitment, and will — regardless of the path you choose — show you what left you have to learn before you can take the next step after that.

Just how my mentor Dan Pena has said, "Just f-ing do it."

There will be challenges, but our learning only comes from the challenges and difficult times we face. Difficult times allow us to stretch, making us stronger. How are you meant to decide you are going to succeed at something if you don't *try* it first?

And how can you say you really did try, if you were not *fully* committed?

You can't. Therefore, you need to commit to trying it out before you decide whether you are going to succeed at this new venture or not.

All too often, we say we can't do things that we know we could. We only consider the fact that it might be hard, or it might not be enjoyable. Nonetheless, we *could* still complete these tasks. We just don't *want* too.

Or, we *think* we don't want to. We don't really know because we haven't actually tried it yet.

People discover they are good at things they never expected all the time. But, how were they ever going to find out they were good at it if they never tried in the first place? They wouldn't, and it would just be a talent wasted.

So, try everything! Anything you can think of that you think you might enjoy, just give it a shot.

Never consider whether you are good enough, smart enough, or anything enough when thinking whether to try something or not. Only consider whether you would *enjoy* the activity or not.

A wild example would be if you wanted to learn how to speak well on a stage, but you believe you are not good enough to be a speaker. Maybe you think you are uncoordinated, or you are not strong enough. You have to drive those limiting beliefs out of your head and ask yourself one question:

What would I **need to do** *to be a Speaker?*

By thinking this way, you can qualify yourself for anything in your head, and you don't need to seek verification from anyone else. You can apply this to every area of your life.

3. BUILD A HIGH-INCOME SKILLSET!

The number one mistake people make when developing their high-income skill set is they go too fast, and they think they've just got it. Thing is, it's not about building a set of skills but building a skill, mastering it, and then stacking another skill set "brick by brick," one by one, mastering the art in each as you experience and understand it.

You don't set out to build a whole wall. You don't say, "I am going to build the biggest, baddest, greatest wall that's ever been built." No, you don't start there; rather, you say, "I'm going to lay this brick as perfectly as a brick can be laid." And you move forward.

Succeed with one high income skill before you jump into a new one.

You need a high-income skill before you proceed with anything. And of course, you don't need just one; you need a stack of skill sets, but to start from somewhere, your one high-income skill should be the only thing that stands apart from all those other skills you possess.

Once you are successful in your high income skill then you can stack on another high income skill set. If you think you have not built a high income skill, then find one, seek out a mentor, or go to my free master class: www.thequantumastercoach.com/freemasterclass.

Once you do build your high-income skill, then you need to have a learning attitude. You should always be absorbing information.

If you are surrounding yourself with the correct type of people, you will naturally gather knowledge as you move through life. If you have any mentors in your life that you look up to, whose opinion you trust, you should be asking as many questions as you can.

For those of you who don't have a mentor, you should take steps to find yourself one. Having someone close to you, in your industry, who knows what they are doing, can be the difference between your overall success and failure.

Any failures along your way should not be viewed as such. Instead, consider them learning curves and be happy that they happened. You will not walk a perfect path, and you will overcome hurdles along the way.

Some of these hurdles you will leap over, and some you will clamber over, but you will make it over nonetheless as long as you persevere. You will learn from every one of these hurdles, and after every one you pass, you will be better.

4. A BURNING DESIRE TO SOLVE THE PROBLEM!

If you have an issue in your life or you are trying to help someone else with an issue in their life, you must engross yourself within the problem to truly know how to fix it.

You have to see the problem in its entirety because to fix a problem, you must fix it from the root. And to find the root of a problem, you must understand it in its fullest capacity.

Everyone loves rewards, but not many of us like the challenges we face in order to gain them. We shy away from the hard work out of the fear that it will be too difficult, or that we will fail before ever receiving any sort of reward for our efforts.

Well, why not just try loving the challenge? Then, it doesn't matter if there is any sort of reward or not, you can just be happy with the fact that you enjoyed the challenge itself.

5. SCRIPT YOUR DAY. DON'T SCHEDULE IT!

Always know your destination by scripting your day. Don't just schedule it.

This is done effectively through the creation of everyday goals:

DIGS, MIGS, YIGS, AND 5YIGS.

What am I talking about?

- Daily Income Goals
- Monthly Income Goals
- Yearly Income Goals
- 5 Yearly Income Goals

These are the goals you need to set and write down. You will be working towards these goals all the time. Think of them as a way of tracking your progress. Be realistic when setting them, and then if you don't hit one of them, evaluate why you didn't. This will help you to hit your targets in the future.

6. FANTASIZE WHAT YOU REALLY WANT IN DETAIL!

When you daydream your goals, how far into detail do you go?

It's likely there are one or two different scenarios you usually picture. Maybe one is a luxury house, and another is you driving the car you really want. Well, you need to go deeper than that.

This one is best experienced as a type of meditation exercise:

Make sure you have at least 5-10 minutes to complete this. Find a quiet place and sit down. Relax yourself and your mind.

Now, think about living your dream life. Think about where you are. Are you abroad? Can you feel the warm air on your face? Think about what you see around you — a luxury yacht, maybe?

Maybe you look down and see your expensive outfit, and you feel the premium fabric. Maybe you notice you're wearing a very expensive watch? Maybe your beautiful wife calls you over to be with her and the kids. They are all wearing expensive clothes too, and you are all healthy and happy.

Whatever your dream is, picture it in your brain, then step into that picture and live it.

Experience all the feelings and emotions that go with it. Don't just look at the car, think about how it makes you *feel* to look at that car. Do you feel pride, excitement, or self-worth? Perhaps you feel a combination of these?

There are no right or wrong answers. There is only your dream and your experience.

7. BE UNREASONABLE!

People around you expect you to be 'reasonable' with your ambitions. They don't want to see you aim for any goal too high because well, God forbid you might actually reach it, and then you would have outperformed them.

This is what makes people scared to go for ideas they believe are bigger than themselves. They think that because everyone else thinks they can't achieve these goals that they have no right to maintain them. So, they drop their ambitions and aim lower.

But, to get where you want to be and truly make yourself a success, you have to be unreasonable. Be unreasonable in the sense that you will not listen to any sort of idea that suggests you can't do something.

Without unreasonable people, we would not have any of the major innovations we have today. If every person who ever invented something listened to negative input from other people all the time, we wouldn't have cars, electricity, the iPhone, or anything remotely close.

You have to be unreasonable to be heard.

8. PAY ATTENTION TO YOUR IDENTITY!

What story are you giving yourself? What identity are you giving yourself?

What do you really think of yourself? Because your today and tomorrow will be exactly what you think of yourself.

The way you feel is decided by how you feel about yourself, not how anyone else feels about you.

You might take those views into consideration, and they might affect how you feel about yourself, but it is ultimately you who decides. This is why you need to learn to never take other people's views into consideration when evaluating yourself. You need your view to be completely yours and controlled by only you.

Only then can you feel what you actually feel about yourself and understand it fully.

When you begin to understand your own identity and why it is the way it is, you can begin to understand how to apply it to your life and start to make things work.

9. FIND THE GAP IN THE MARKETPLACE AND ADD VALUE FIRST BEFORE ASKING FOR MONEY!

You can't go to a bank and just ask for some money. First, you have to make a deposit. If you deposit and withdraw immediately, you also fail. Same as in a marketplace: You can't ask for money before **adding value** first, helping people in advance, while continuing to deliver some value … all before you ask for any money. This is one thing that has made me a millionaire.

Whenever I've noticed a gap in the marketplace, I added value first and kept adding more value until I asked for the money, instantly building the trust and connection. Now, most people don't do that, all because it requires a confident entrepreneurial mindset. This is why, in the first section of this book, I emphasize mindset so much.

When you add value first to solve an individual's problem, the market will come to you by itself. Because you've positioned yourself as an expert.

You are not selling your time, your knowledge, or *your expertise; rather, you are selling the value of the outcome you deliver.*

Finding a gap in any marketplace is challenging, but it becomes easier when you master a skill set and solve the problem of your audience, as your ethical responsibility.

When you can solve a common problem and sell the solution, you stand to become a very rich man.

When you solve someone else's problem, and you sell them a solution, you are selling them convenience. You are providing a convenient alternative to what they already do. People are prepared to pay a lot of money for such convenience.

Finding a gap in any marketplace is challenging. We live in a saturated world of people and businesses that seem to have already thought of everything. It can be frustrating when you think you've found a gap in the market only to discover someone else has already thought of it. But, when you find that gap, and you bridge it beautifully, people will walk over to it, use your solution, and pay top dollar to do so.

Seems extreme, but if you look at your business this way, you will feel obliged to take care of it and ensure it gets the exercise it needs. By taking care of your business in this way, you will see immense improvements in your sales capabilities.

10. YOUR ENVIRONMENT IS MORE POWERFUL THAN YOUR WILLPOWER!

Who are you surrounding yourself with?

I have been asked this question multiple times: "John, what should I do if I have toxic people around me?" My answer is always, "Quit on them."

Then they ask, "Well, what if they're family? What if I love them?" And I say, "Quit on them, because if they are toxic and stopping you from having the life you want, the dreams you want, then you need to quit on those people."

When I was struggling with my finances and career, I was not developing my skills further because I was in the wrong environment.

I was being dragged down by those around me until, at one point in my life, I started to see success and notice the difference in how I was living. I cut off all the people who were toxic, including my social media and any other friends whom I didn't need or who could waste my time.

I was living my life for them rather than for myself, doing things so I would look cool in their eyes. This was one of the biggest obstacles in my life and took some time to overcome.

You cannot decide you are not good enough to do something or that it is not going to work if you have not put 100% of your effort into trying it for a decent amount of time. You cannot go 'half-in' and then claim it's not going to be successful because this is just you doubting yourself.

Be thankful for your failures as they will stretch you and show you who you are. They will show you how you deal with adversity and how you pick yourself up after a knockdown. You will build your success on these failures because you are teaching yourself what doesn't work.

Treat people who criticize you in the same way. Others might tell you that you're not good enough or that you're not ready, but you only ever have to trust yourself. If you believe that you are good enough or that you are ready now, then go for it. Your own opinion of yourself is the only one that matters.

So, whenever you do take on a new task or attempt to learn a new skill, ask yourself whether you're surrounded by the right environment. If not, then cut those people off, change your surroundings, change your environment, and declutter your mind and space of what's not supporting you. Only you will know whether or not you actually tried your best, so make sure you can ask yourself this question and honestly answer with a yes.

"Your environment is more powerful than your willpower."

11. BUILD A SCALABLE INCOME!

Many people come to me and ask how they can scale their business. There are only three ways to scale your business, all of which I learned from one of my mentors, marketing godfather Jay Abraham.

Just thinking of your marketing and business activities as falling in one of these three categories will help keep you focused and will quickly give you a boost in revenues and profits.

1. Increase the number of clients; turn more new prospects into paying customers.
2. Increase the average transaction; get each client to buy more at each purchase.
3. Increase the frequency that the average client buys from you; get each customer to buy from you more often.

It would be nice for me to give examples of each category, but I think it's much more powerful for you to take an hour and brainstorm ways to increase business and then to see in which of these three your ideas fall into.

Doing this will help cement in this concept. When I learned this from The Mentors' Mentor Jay Abraham, I applied it in my business. It has taken all my businesses from nowhere to a solid 7 figures.

Most people, including me, think that increasing business is a complex giant burden consisting of thousands of possible tactics one can try. However, focusing on only three business-building categories throughout our business lives doesn't seem so bad right?

When I started doing business consulting, I was hungry to learn more about how to have growth in my business so I could provide this for my clients. I was going from seminars to masterminds when I learned that there are three important pillars to consider for your business growth.

1. Enticing: Being able to predictably and consistently attract new quality leads and generate new business.
2. Preserving: Increasing the stick rate of each customer and enhancing the relationship customers have with your business.
3. Enhancing: Maximizing the value your business generates for the customer.

Most struggling entrepreneurs are weak in either one or a blend of these three pillars. As you will see, these pillars work together to create a strong, sustainable, and scalable business. If any of these pillars are weak, you are looking at an unbalanced business.

12. MARKET COMES FIRST — GIVE PEOPLE WHAT THEY WANT!

The market you sell to is more important than the products or services you sell. Give them what they want. That will solve their problem and end up giving them a value of the outcome they wanted.

The number one reason people fail is because they spend so much time creating the perfect product without even knowing if there's a market for what they offer. Big mistake.

The absolute key to your Internet success anytime you decide to begin ANY money-making project online is effective market research.

Remember, people don't buy from you because they understand what you sell — they buy from you because they feel understood. Too many times, I have been guilty of making that mistake.

In the beginning of my marketing career, I had a whole lot more losing business ideas than winners. However, as I've refined my market research techniques over the years, my rate of success has improved exponentially.

As a result, I've enjoyed a drastically improved income as well. Research your market and find out what people want and are willing to buy. Not what you think they might buy, not what you think they should buy, but what they're actually spending money on already.

Ask yourself:

Is the market already buying something similar to what I'm thinking of selling?

Is this a market where people buy, or is this a market of people who have no money and are looking for something free?

Is the market big enough?

Are there existing partners in the market I can form a joint venture with?

Am I able to reach these buyers?

Am I going to be able to drive traffic to my website and get them to buy my products?

Start with a topic that has a future to it. A lot of Internet entrepreneurs fail because they choose a niche without a lot of back-end potential. They choose a niche that doesn't have legs to stand on its own and won't support additional selling opportunities beyond the first sale.

Start with a market that has a viable future to it. Identify niches where people have money and are used to spending it on products within that niche — for example, golfers. People who are into golf are fanatical about improving their game, and they're willing to plop down a good chunk of change to buy the latest gadgets, read the latest books, watch the latest videos, you name it, just to shave one stroke off their score.

Sell something that is already proven to sell. If you want to find out where money is being made, look no further than where money is being spent.

13. BELIEVE IN YOUR PRODUCT AND SERVICES MORE THAN ANYONE ELSE!

It is very important you believe this. This concept is vital.

You have to believe in your product.

You cannot be half-invested. You cannot have any doubt in your mind that your product is the best solution to the problem you are solving. There cannot be a shred of uncertainty when you explain to people why they *need* your product.

Listen, no one else is going to sell your product for you, are they? No.

So, you have to get good at selling. It's something you can't really get around.

(You could hire a sales team if you wanted to, but you should still be good at sales because you need to know if they are doing a good job or not.)

To learn the art of sales, you can take structured courses, learn from a mentor, or just go out there and practice. I recommend all three.

But remember, even if you become a top-class salesman, you will struggle to sell something you don't believe in fully. So that's why it's crucial you fully understand and push your product to its highest potential.

You have to believe that if you do not sell your product in some way or another, that it will die and never see the light of day. View your product or service as a living, breathing animal. It needs exercise to survive or else it will wither away and die.

14. LEVERAGE THE TIME AND ENERGY OF OTHERS!

Like I mention in this book multiple times, the only two commodities you have are Time and Energy, so in order to become successful and scale faster, you would need to leverage other's people time and energy.

There are exactly twenty-four hours a day. Regardless of what you do within these hours, there's still just twenty-four hours. There is no added hour; thus, you will never be able to work 25 hours in a single day. So how do you maximize your income in your business (irrespective of what stage it is currently) if you do not have much time?

You must make use of other people's time. Outsourcing has made me a multimillionaire; I wouldn't have been this accomplished if I hadn't learned and used the power of allocating work to other people.

Don't be mistaken. I also do work. But to me, my work isn't that much of a work. I love what I do. My products, my customers, and growing my businesses are so dear to me. But I outsource and delegate whatever work it is I don't like to others who are experts in it. Completion of the job becomes theirs, not mine.

I also invest part of my time in doing twenty percent of the valuable tasks that would make the work easier. Compared to the construction worker across the street, I don't work nearly as hard as people who make little incomes compared to me.

Perhaps you are wondering if I am a techie. No, I am not. I have no knowledge of any programming or any technology-related stuff. I also don't know WordPress. Honestly, my time is much more valuable than that. I don't have any interest in doing that nerd code stuff. I can easily go online and find someone to do this stuff for me.

It is essential you consider outsourcing if you really want to maximize your profits. You will later find that paying other people to do the work in your business that you don't enjoy becomes one of the greatest feelings in life. This will help you free up your time to do only the important things you really want to do.

When you do this, a time will come eventually that your business will be like mine. I don't have much that I do in regards to the daily operation of my business.

15. CREATE MULTIPLE INCOME STREAMS IN ONE BUSINESS. DON'T CREATE MANY DIVERSIFIED BUSINESSES!

Many entrepreneurs have taken the wrong way in this part, and it is an essential part of a business. In my past several years in business, I have seen many entrepreneurs come and go due to misunderstanding this one.

There are many financial gurus that encourage entrepreneurs to build multiple streams of income. It's a very great concept. There is a big debate between gurus about it and both are convincing in their side. However, you and I are not living in the same economy in which we were born. Many things have changed.

We have entered into a new economy: one of "air," and a lot of things are going to change from here on out. It is important for you to create your own universe, your own omnichannel that has diversified income within it.

This simply means to not put all of your eggs in one basket. You have to create more baskets within your universe, and before one source of income dries up, you must have three to five more baskets to diversify your income within your universe. Then, you can always fall back on another stream of income.

A lot of people get the wrong idea about this concept, however. Any entrepreneurs trying to make money with ten completely different businesses will eventually result in disaster. It will cause a whole lot of confusion. All you really need is multiple streams of income within a business.

Doing it this way gives you a better chance of succeeding. You'll never reach a stage of confusing success because you have a million little things going on. It is better to sell to one market and serve the needs of a particular group of targeted people.

Even though there are a lot of opportunities everywhere on the Internet, instead of hurdling from one market to another, pursuing every idea you come up with (and driving yourself crazy in the process), I suggest you squeeze as much money as you can out of a particular market.

Spend every avenue you have for making money within your current market, and there is an assurance that you'll make more money than you ever would by moving from one market to another. Provide different products for your clients to buy, and also find several sources of traffic to drive to your website.

When you begin to understand your buyers in the market. the more you gain experience in that market. And that automatically increases the amount of income you'll earn. Inside your initial market, you can create as many ways of making money as you desire.

Although I have multiple businesses in multiple markets, it has been successful because I have systems in place. I have other associates in those niches, and I have created an idea that I can replicate. But I started with multiple businesses in ONE market. I advise you to do the same.

Be well established in one thing as big as you can before you move onto something else. Give it your all, and you'll make five to ten times more money.

16. POSITION YOUR BUSINESS FOR AUTOMATIC GROWTH!

This is one of the most important processes, as many people try to do everything on their own. And when they do, they then struggle in managing their time and energy, which prevents them from hitting their daily, weekly, monthly, and yearly goals.

During the process of developing your business, you should make sure to position your business in as many ways as possible to spontaneously make money for you.

Do you have a business online that is making you money? Try and figure out the steps you took to make the money you are making now. Note the crucial activities responsible for making you money, then introduce technology or people to repeat those processes again and again.

Get some technology and the right people in your team to leverage your income for automatic growth. There are many inexpensive solutions in the marketplace, and as compared to the early days, it has been easier to scale than ever before.

A technique I have used that has made me a lot of money: Do more of what works instead of trying to fix what's broken. All you have to do is to focus on modifying the things that bring you the greatest income, so you can duplicate and multiply the results. Automate your business as much as you can.

Not everyone will understand what you do and how you make your money; most of your friends and family won't understand. Just focus on showing them the results, and the numbers will speak louder themselves.

So, commit first and decide later. Rest assured, if you use chapter nine as your formula for success, you will succeed.

You can and will do so. It's never too late to start.

17. CREATE A MASSIVE MOVEMENT!

When you know what solution you are going to provide to the marketplace and you go all the way in, it's time for you to create a massive movement.

Now your success is not about you anymore; it's about people. The moment you think this way, you become a great leader.

I learned this example from the great Martin Luther King. He created a movement in order to solve a problem until that brings the solution brings a movement that brings a transformation cycle in life.

I was in a ClickFunnels conference held by Russel Brunson and left inspired by how he has created a massive movement of entrepreneurs by creating a platform where they can bring their ideas to the table to create a blue ocean strategy.

Look at the examples of Jim Rohn, Napoleon Hill, Bob Proctor, Tony Robbins … it was no longer about their own success but that they wanted to see the success of others. This has inspired me the most.

18. CREATE AN IDENTITY SHIFT FOR YOUR CLIENT!

Don't focus on just creating ideas, because ideas don't solve the problem. Instead, giving your client a breakthrough and shifting their identity is what is going to break the biggest bank in your career.

In my career working as a business consultant, I saw many people come to me with brilliant new Uber ideas or new Facebook ideas, but I told them to follow the example of McDonald's — who made them big is Ray Kroc.

Same example with Tesla, which was founded by Martin Eberhard. But who really solved the problem in the marketplace, who really took that company to another level was Elon Musk. Same with Steve Jobs who said *I am going to make this phone so sexy and lucrative that people are going to lick the buttons of this phone.*

They will feel an identity shiftn what he did for Apple. Take the example of Facebook — it was initially an idea of someone else, but it was Mark Zuckerberg who took it and created a new identity for their clients to share, network, find, and even do business.

Each of these entrepreneurs has created an identity shift for their client, rather than remaining focused on ideas or content alone. The purpose of the business is not to give only content or product or service, but to give your client Version 2.0 (the identity shift).

Whenever someone walks into a store to buy new, expensive, or beautiful clothes, it is because that person wants the identity *I* status. As an entrepreneur, if you learn to offer an identity shift to your client, you will create massive value in the marketplace.

19. BE TRANSPARENT!

When I was studying the top 1% of entrepreneurs, I was astonished to find one thing — one very simple thing among all of them — which was they were great, long-lasting influencers.

And the only thing which was common among all of them was that they were completely transparent with their raving fans, bringing immediate trust to their audience and building instant rapport and relationship.

People like anything which is the purest form of itself. If you are the purest form of yourself, just being you, then more clients are going to trust you and will build instant rapport with you. Transparency is not only important, but has become the number one rule for any successful brand in my book.

A buyer is a buyer and always a buyer because once you have provided massive value to your customer, you are signing that customer for a long-term relationship. Since you have given them an identity shift, they are transformed into someone they always wanted to be.

This is a moment where you can sell them another piece of your valuable work. When you are transparent, it opens you to your true self-worth, and when you find your true self-worth, you open to your real creativity.

You see, we all have creativity inside of us, but part of us believes we don't. And then that becomes the decision, which causes limitations in our life, and that becomes part of the limiting belief.

If I were to, say, only follow one piece of the rule as being transparent, this will allow you to learn, grow, and evolve. And when you are stretching, it is always going to make you more dominant and powerful.

20. ASK THESE 3 POWERFUL QUESTIONS!

1. What works?
2. What doesn't work?
3. What am I doing right now?

My client has taken her company from 2 million to 64 million just by answering these questions for herself each and every day.

If something is not working with a product, service, or client, just follow up with the customer! Even if it has nothing to do with your client, contact them to ask them why they did not buy your product or service. Ask them what went wrong in their purchasing experience.

If you believe in your product or service, then never give up on it! This is one of the major mistakes most big companies make. The reason they are struggling in scaling their business is because they are not following up with their clients!

Statistics show that 86% of deals close upon follow up, 11% are never closed, and only 3% are closed upon the first offer. It all comes down to developing yourself through these three powerful questions.

"The doors will be open to those who are bold enough to knock."

- Tony Gaskins

TEN

What The Hell Am I Suppossed To Do Now?

To become the person you truly want to be, you need to first let go of the person you once were. You can't grow and evolve by clinging to former versions of yourself.

My story is being told, so *you* can finally start creating your own. And who knows, you might tell yours to the world one day.

Important: I highly recommend you read chapter 9 if you have not already before jumping into this section.

We think we don't need a mentor or someone's help, or we may be afraid to change because we are too comfortable in our comfort zone. I have given examples of how all successful people have one thing in common— they are constantly moving and are never stuck in their comfort zone — how can you move? What can drive you? What is your motivator to come out of your comfort zone? Pain or pleasure? And what needs to change now?

Now that you've learned about the financial stages, this section teaches you how to implement the data and actually get there.

This is the most important section, as practical application means more than theory ever could. And considering that you've read the first chapters of this book, you're probably thinking, *What the hell am I supposed to do now?* Well, now is the time for action. And now is the moment to integrate the previous steps I've taught you into your life.

So how do you become successful like those you admire? To be the change you want to see and experience a major shift in mentality and levels of success, you need to emulate those who you admire. That's why these rules were written.

By now, you've got valuable insights into how the wealthy and elite — the 1% — operate on a daily basis. You're excited, rallied up, ready to bulldoze your way to success, but you're stuck at the starting line thinking, "Where do I begin?"

I wanted to do things differently with this book. That's why *Rewiring Your Success* is more than just ideas. It's philosophies about lifestyle, income, and mindset. Too many personal growth books fill you with ideas but rarely do anything to actually tell you how to implement them.

They get you pumped up, blood flowing and excited beyond belief, but you don't move an inch. Your life remains exactly as it was before you started reading. Or even worse, you finish the book even more lost and confused than before you started.

My mission has always been to steer away from confusion and doubt and lead you into action. So when I started writing, I said to myself: "If

I'm going to do this, I'm going to do it right." If I was going to write a book, I was going to do it my way — the John Qreshi way.

Do you remember when you started reading, how I said you might not find ALL the answers you're looking for? But what you will find are the tools and strategies to carve a life of brilliance. But above all, if there's one thing I want you to take away, it's this: Question everything. Think differently.

If you do so, you can live a truly exceptional life.

I tend not to hold back, putting everything on the table as bluntly as possible. But it comes from a place of caring. Because I don't want you to fail, and you need to understand the reality of the world. My failures, flaws, mistakes, and successes are exposed for you to learn from in the most authentic way possible. And I do hope you appreciate the results.

But if I wasn't brutally honest and in your face, what type of mentor would I be? Not a very good one. So as we come to the end of this book, if you understand the secrets of success and wealth, then my job is done. But above all, I want you to understand that there's a new path for you if you choose. A new life. A new mindset and a fresh way of thinking. I want you to see the world with bright eyes.

So from this section until the last chapter, you will learn what to do next.

Ask yourself, what is really missing in your life? And ask yourself what needs to change now?

Go back to chapter nine. Check which things you have not been following or doing, and then ask yourself these three powerful questions:

1. What do I really want?
2. What have I done about it in the past? And how has it been working for me?
3. What needs to change now? What actions am I going to take to move towards my goal? In other words, what is my ultimate next step?

So, if you haven't guessed what time it is now, allow me to enlighten you: Now, it's time for action. I can't hold your hand and force you to do what's necessary to succeed. It's up to YOU to take the bull by the horns, get up off your ass, and move.

Don't even think about putting this book down without at least taking some steps in the right direction. If you want to succeed, you need to start moving, no matter how small the steps. Hell, even if you're crawling towards your goal, it's better than staying still.

You might read this, put it back on the shelf, and not do a damn thing with it in your own life. You may even bring it up with your friends and talk about all the great advice it has to offer. But you won't take the necessary steps to change. Then, it simply becomes another book, collecting dust as the years pass by.

I don't want this to happen to you. I don't want you to be like the other 99%.

And yes, I know, change is never easy. But it's necessary. But don't attack your dreams and think you'll succeed by doing everything alone. We all need help and guidance. It's why I wrote this book.

You might say, "I'll do whatever it takes to find success." But are you truly committed?

If you answered yes, know this: Commitment requires structure. Without structure, commitment can't be measured as amounting to anything at all. So I created an exclusive online training to help you structure your commitment and snowball your success. To gain access, go to www.quantumastercoach.com/freemasterclass.

In this exclusive members-only area, I give all my recommendations for anyone who wants to increase their income as fast as possible. I also talk about what I would do differently if I had to start life over from zero. You don't want to miss this.

Consider this. If you're trying to lose weight, telling other people how committed you are to it won't do a damn thing. It's not going to melt the pounds off. Why? Because you haven't tracked your calories, scheduled your workouts, recorded your weigh-ins, or even gotten a personal trainer. THAT is structure, and structure will be the difference between whether you win and achieve your goals, or you don't.

So now, it's time for the good and bad news. The bad news is, the clock has started ticking. The countdown is on now that you've finished chapter 9. The good news? You have NO reason not to get up off your butt and attack the day. Just start moving!

Remember when I said crawling is better than not moving at all? You need to start taking some small form of action as soon as possible. I recommend writing it down within 24 hours. In fact, you should be doing it right now. Jot down your goals and start taking the necessary steps to reach them.

The clock is ticking. Every second that goes by increases the chances of this book becoming another wasted investment. Another dust collector. Another volume you've decided wasn't worth your energy because you can't get up and take action.

And that's an unethical thing to do to yourself because, with all this suffering, you've already come this far, all to become more, to learn, to grow, and to evolve more … all to live the life you've most desired.

In fact, you probably would have been better off not reading this book at all if you're not going to act. Because I've literally given you the knowledge and the steps to success. So if you've read this much and you can't get moving, it's up to you to deal with the guilt and regret. I've shown you the HOW. Now you need to manifest your dreams. Only you are responsible. Tick tock.

Only 0.00003% of the entire world's population are billionaires. That's 2,604 people. And one-quarter of them are from the U.S.

But here's the thing. Everyone makes becoming wealthy seem more complex than it really is. You'll find once you change your mindset and structure your days, weeks, and months, money finds you. Don't follow what everyone else does. Learn from the wealthy and elite, follow their habits, and you'll find success too.

It's easy to look at the wealthy with envy and disdain. But remember, that's your lower self talking. Your lack of confidence in yourself is bringing out your jealousy. Instead of being angry, ask yourself what it takes to reach their level. Enter their minds and use them as ammunition to blast your own trail to the stars. Ask yourself, "How did they do it?" You'll soon find that you can too.

Do you want to be a millionaire? Does that even cut it in today's world? You might dream of earning billions. Either way, the first step is to realize that it's far from impossible. In fact, if you commit, it's highly doable.

Just look back at history. It's been done by countless people over and over again. They are no different from you. The only difference is the one you create in your mind. Oprah Winfrey, Jim Rohn, Tony Robbins,

Daymond John, Kevin O'Leary, Mark Cuban, and Jeff Bezos were each flat broke at one time in their lives, then all went on to become billionaires.

Of course, the first step is to first become a millionaire. So let's focus on that.

Do you know what happens if you double a penny every day for 30 days? One penny becomes two, two becomes four, four becomes eight, and so on. Well, after 30 days, you'd be sitting on more than 5 million dollars.

How many times would you have to fold a piece of paper for its thickness to reach the moon? For the average sheet, 10 folds gives you 3 feet of thickness. 20 folds could reach an airplane cruising altitude. If you fold the same sheet 42 times, you could climb it to the moon. And 53 folds? You'd literally reach the ends of the known universe.

This is known as the compound or snowball effect. It's exponential growth. When you start walking, one step becomes two, two becomes four, and so on. But the point is, in business, there are no limits to your growth like there is when folding paper.

And it's how every billionaire you know made their riches. For Steve Jobs, it was scaling Apple to new heights. For Zuckerberg, Facebook skyrocketed him into the billions.

Small, well-made choices throughout the years lead to the compound effect. But the best part is, even though the results you reap are massive, the steps are small and incremental. They don't feel life-changing at all. Which means ANYONE can take them. And this strategy works for your business career, health, relationships, or anything you can think of!

And while these changes take time to show results, it's the simplicity of it that makes the compound effect so powerful.

So why wait any longer? Starting today, I want you to start compounding, taking small steps to success through constant effort. No matter how small. Just start moving. Your choice to keep moving forward will make the difference between you and the rest of the average individuals all over the world. After all, life is a series of choices, and you're defined by the ones you make. But if you play your cards right, the next turn of a comer could lead you to the stars and beyond.

Your choices until now have crafted your reality. Think about it. Every behavior and action begins with a choice. And behaviors then go on to become habits. Make the wrong choice, and you could suffer. Continually make the right choices, and they'll form into lifelong habits to help you excel.

I want you to start becoming acutely aware of the choices you make. Are they leading you away from your goals or towards them? If you're more aware, you can make better decisions for yourself, your career, and your family. Self-awareness is key.

You need to start keeping tabs on everything. You need to monitor every choice you make. Trying to pay off a loan? Every penny you make must be accounted for. Trying to lose weight? Every calorie should be recorded. Tracking is a way to measure and quantify your progress, as well as bring you clarity that you're moving in the right direction.

So start tracking your life with the intention of becoming a winner. Every day, write down your metrics, goals, actions, and next steps. Be committed and consistent. There's a genius in simplicity, and that's what the magic of compounding is all about.

Never neglect the small actions that lead to massive results. And remember this: To live like the 1%, you need to be willing to do what the 99% aren't. So when you're feeling tired, lazy, or unmotivated, keep that thought in the back of your mind and get moving.

But it's vital you start today. If you're still confused about where to go from here, I'm telling you right now: Take out your pen and paper, Excel sheet, or whatever you choose, pick one habit and start tracking it. It will work in your favor the sooner you do so.

The added benefit of the compound effect is that it teaches you patience. It teaches you not to expect instant results, but instead to trust in the process that you're moving in the right direction. This will help ensure you don't fall off the wagon. We live in a world where we expect everything at the snap of our fingers. The sooner you can rid yourself of this short-minded mentality, the more successful you'll be.

And the compound effect helps you nurture this trait until you make practice a part of your daily life. Repetition of action breeds skill. Skill breeds confidence and self-esteem. And self-esteem is the foundation for success.

Do you think your favorite athlete is doing anything less than repeating the same drills, eating the same meals, and practicing the same movements? It's discipline and confidence that's going to set you apart from the rest of the non-achievers in the world. So start tracking. Keep practicing and build rock-solid discipline to make this year, and all the years to come, the best of your life.

The clock is still ticking. Don't even think about waiting another minute to start taking action. Remember that over-analysis leads to paralysis. Stop thinking and start doing, working in the direction of your goals until your old life is nothing but a distant memory.

The countdown is on. 3, 2, 1 … You know what to do!

"Someone's opinion of you doesn't have to become your reality."

- Les Brown

ELEVEN

The Power Of Your Identity

I have talked about your identity often. And it's one of the core pillars of successful people. Now, it's not "fake it till you make it;" rather, it's the identity you consciously give to yourself.

If you remember, I started the first chapter of this book with the story you are telling yourself. It's about the identity you're giving to yourself. If deep inside, you wake up angry or upset or thinking, "I am screwed," then your identity is going to massively reflect this upon your unconscious mind.

And it will reflect immediately what you think of yourself. Now, can one find an identity with arrogance? Will it work? A person might think it would work, but there are many consequences of being arrogant.

Rejecting your own insecurities comes with a huge price. When you are arrogant, you are hiding your true self. And as time passes, you become more and more insecure about yourself.

I am talking about the identity that you give to yourself of who you believe you are. And that simply cannot be done if you have not read the book completely.

Your identity is a belief you give to yourself. If someone asks me to give them the magic pill, this is one of the most powerful magic pills to discover. Discover what identity you really want to give to yourself, and your life will immediately reflect upon it.

When I say immediately, I mean this can sometimes happen in seconds.

When I was learning how to speak on stages, the most important part was anchoring. Anchoring is a tactic where you recall a time when you were totally confident. You feel what you felt at that time, see what you saw, and you would hear what you heard. And when you are in that state, you squeeze your thumb or your ear, which helps you to anchor into that feeling.

So when you are going on stage, you anchor into that part of your body, and then you are in that state. Then you are confident.

This is a good example of giving yourself an identity.

Now, why does every speaker do this anchoring before going to perform in front of a massive audience, teach a training, or perform? It's because he/she wants to bring results or perform or bring an outcome for himself/herself and all those people.

Same as if you are working in a professional environment. If you can give yourself a powerful identity, then your meeting will reflect that, but if you give yourself a shitty identity, your presentation or meeting will showcase that as well.

The words we say about ourselves and to ourselves change our beliefs about who we are as individuals. The words we use can create limiting beliefs or build us up to reach our dreams. There is no one we talk to more than ourselves, so we need to learn to be kind to ourselves in order to shape a better life. A life we can truly love and adore. A life that loves us back!

Think about how you describe yourself to others. If you focus on negatives and past failures, you start to hone in those pieces of your story, instead of looking toward the future and focusing on your positives.

Limiting beliefs can hold you back from making important decisions and cause you to miss out on opportunities. They cause you to focus on the negative aspects provided by circumstance instead of looking for a solution.

Beliefs are made up of words, but by changing one word, you begin to change what you believe to be true.

Transform your influence by transforming your language.

The words we use become habitual, and by changing the language we use, we can change our emotional states permanently. Think about the way you feel, and tum those feelings into words to experience a deeper connection to your feelings, making them more pleasurable or painful. We label experiences through our words and shape those experiences in our minds based on our personal views.

Instead of saying, "I can't do this because I am not smart or I am poor or I can't afford it," try saying, "How can I do that? How can I make it happen? How can I afford it?"

The right question opens your mind and rewires it. *A statement closes your mind.*

It's often easier to think up more intense words for negative thoughts and feelings, and much harder to think of powerful words for positive thoughts. Words are the building blocks that will shape your experiences and change our way of thinking. So, instead, think of intense words for positive emotions.

Think of three words you habitually use when describing negative emotions, and then find three alternatives that are more empowering. More positive. More aligned with the identity you can use to support your professional offerings to your clients. As I've said before, people will believe what is pure. They will support you when they feel your true identity in your work!

Labels create feelings, and giving yourself the power to label something as a positive will expand your view on life, thus allowing positivity to flow. That becomes your identity.

Most of the stress we feel in our daily lives is created by our reactions to situations, instead of the actual circumstances of the situation. By conditioning your language and the way you speak and think about your life, you create an environment that supports you. When you consistently speak out loud with emotional intensity, you will create your own experiences and shape your own life.

One of the most powerful self-help solutions is practicing invocation — or an affirming phrase as a chant. For example, "I am happy and grateful now that money comes to me in increasing quantities through multiple sources on a continuous basis." Or, "I am the leader. I will lead not follow," and, "I will create, and I am the co-creator of my life."

By incorporating these mantras into the first 60 seconds of your day, you are giving your unconscious mind a new identity, and you will start to see a change in the way you feel, think about yourself, and view the world.

Your entire day will be different, all around you, as a whole. Speak phrases like these out loud with absolute certainty and in repetition until you believe what you are saying. You are engaging the focus of your emotions and your body to activate your beliefs.

You can use this exercise as a way to deeply instill your personal identity. As a means of cementing in your identity — not only on an individual level, but in how you stand out to dominate your marketplace. All of which we will talk about in the next chapter.

* * *

Guess who?

I was alone.
I was broke.

I was overweight.

I was living in a one-bedroom apartment.

I've read more than seven hundred books in the area of personal development and success. One day, I decided that my life would change, and never again would I settle for anything less than what I ultimately desire and envision for my life.

I started applying all that I'd been learning from books, tapes, and seminars, and within one year, I turned my whole life around. I became a millionaire in less than one year. I live in a mansion. I've put what I've learned in a bunch of tapes and now I want to show YOU how to change your life for the better.

Whose story is it?

Tony Robbins

"My definition of marketing is simple -it's all about educating the marketplace that your business can solve problems, fill voids, or achieve opportunities and goals the way no other business can."

- Jay Abraham

TWELVE

How To Dominate The Marketplace

Competition is for sissies!

How you can truly dominate the marketplace is by solving the problem of your niche, scaling your business by giving consumers the big promise, and by committing to your purpose.

There are two big human motivators: pain and pleasure.

If you solve the problem or take away their pain, it will drive customers, and you will instantly become an authority in the marketplace. The other way to do it is to give people what they need. That instant gratification will give them the pleasure of what they needed.

Let me show you what has made me successful. The first thing you need to do is master a skill set.

Most people, when they go about trying to master any skill set, only actually finish it about 40%, and then they think, "I got it!" After that, they move on to "master" the next one and, at the end of the day, you get Mr. or Ms. "Jack of All Trades, Master of None." That person has zero value in the marketplace.

What I mean by "mastering a skill set" is that you need to have the right tools, strategy, and techniques. Only then can you bring proven results. Once you are able to bring proven results, you will be able to solve big problems for your clients in the marketplace. It is when you can promise your clients big promises and deliver on them that you take this next step. This is when you will finally be able to create scalable income.

This is when you can scale your business. If you want to see how I designed a wealth pyramid and how it looks, then go to
www.quantumastercoach.com/freemasterclass.

When you scale your business, all those services, products, testimonials, solutions, networks, content, results, media, and your achievements become your valuable assets.

This is when you position yourself as an expert in the market. This is when you can diversify your income into high return investments.

When you have high return investments such as bonds or hedge funds, most people do the opposite. Most people jump into scaling their business too fast. When this happens, they grow too thin and then blame things like their clients or bad Facebook ads when their strategy doesn't work.

Most people skip the part where they fully take the time to master a skill set.

I have made this same mistake when buying a house. I thought that by simply buying a house, I would gain financial certainty and be on my way to financial independence. What I found though is that buying the house did not give me the certainty I thought it would.

What I found is that the only way I could move from wanting that certainty and significance in my life would be to continue growing and contributing by mastering each step.

Once you master these, you create your own universe, and everything becomes omni-directional. This is when your universe becomes your powerful personal brand.

Now, I will talk more about personal branding in chapter 19, but the more you create your personal brand, the more you will form your own universe. Your own universe allows you more chances to create a big, blue ocean around you and cut through all the noise of the 1.5 billion websites in the world. It will allow you to stand out more and dominate the marketplace.

You DO NOT need a million followers to do this. You only need 100 true, raving fans. People whose lives you have changed and who will then refer others to you to work with. This is how you grow. This is how you dominate the marketplace!

If you are interested in learning more about how you can truly master skill sets and have scalable income, go to my link for a free masterclass.

"Creating opportunities means looking where others are not."

- Mark Cuban

THIRTEEN

Criticism And Rising Haters Are The Signs Of Success

When you are creating massive movement and change in people's lives by providing some value, product, or services, you will surely have haters. And if you do not have any haters, this means you are not succeeding.

One of my biggest fears was what people would think of me if I tried this or tried that … and it was stopping me from doing absolutely everything. Once I realized that not necessarily everyone would like me, no matter what I did, my job became clear: It was to render the best service I could and to give my best by solving the most difficult problem in the marketplace.

It immediately settled me down to a new level of success, which then allowed me to be able to speak in front of thousands of people on stage.

This is how I was able to scale other people's success and messages out in the marketplace.

My mentor once told me, "Not even Jesus had 100 percent fans. People will always have haters and lovers, so your job is to render the service to those who need you."

And that's your job. To take note of the haters, but also take note of the raving fans that come along with them. And then to keep rising, and do what you feel called to do, regardless!

I see haters who have helped me and hurt me in life; it gives me both, for who I am and get some of my ideas out there.

I believe part of it is because people try to figure out how this guy shows up every single day, what is running him or driving him to produce results.

I will share with you now the five most important points about haters which are important for you to understand and accept:

#1: Haters are coming for you if you make a move, if you write an article on LinkedIn or social media. There are haters coming for you, so know how to handle them.

#2: The hater is not talking to you; rather, the hater is talking to himself/herself. You make them think about themselves.

#3: You've had a victory: You wrote an article, you reached success, you wrote a book … and they are coming for you. You remind them of what they don't do!

#4: They are so stupid because they end up promoting you by hating on you. Let me tell you that nobody promotes me better than my haters. They are the best marketing tool in the world.

#5: Haters are not the people to fear. Who you should be fearful of is YOU if you QUIT on yourself because of haters.

Understand this: haters are trying to bring you down because they are already below you.

At last, when you are getting haters, this is a sign you are becoming successful. So cheer yourself up and continue to be persistent.

"If you do not get the chills when you set your goal, you're not setting big enough goals."

- Jim Rohn

FOURTEEN

What You Can Learn From The Planet's Wealthiest People

I learned this from my mentor Dr. Adriana James and once I understood this, it completely changed the way I see the world: "Money is a mirror. The way you use money is a way of understanding yourself in exactly the same way that a mirror provides a way of seeing yourself. It will only expand who you truly are."

Now, time to talk facts. But be warned, this could shatter everything you thought you knew about business, education, and success in general. You see, all high achieving, hyper-successful people in life — the wealthy and elite — always go against traditional knowledge. I'm talking about the world's most influential people, like Henry Ford, Thomas Edison, Jeff Bezos, Warren Buffet, Bill Gates, Steve Jobs, Fred Smith. The list goes on.

I can personally guarantee that any *truly* successful individual you know has committed to doing what others felt was wrong. They went against the grain, blocked out the negativity, and trailblazed their way to become the pioneers of our generation.

Richard Branson spent his *entire* career hearing people complain that he was doing things the wrong way. He shattered every piece of traditional business wisdom there is. And he's a billionaire, for God's sake. Did I mention he's also the first person to develop a commercial spaceflight?

Yep, Richard Branson is reaching new stars, and you're still listening to conventional advice that will get you *nowhere*. But that's about to change.

You see, throughout my years, I have been told, "Don't even dream of doing that." But looking back, I'm proud to say I did them anyway, because if I hadn't, I wouldn't be sitting here on a large fortune writing this book!

So to understand the type of conventional, negative advice to ignore, I thought I'd recall some common objections I've heard over the years (that you'll hear too). Below is a list of things that people told me that I would not able to do. But, I went ahead and did them anyway.

1. You can't succeed without the right background!
2. You can't be a highly profitable entrepreneur without constant "hustle"!
3. You can't generate millions following your passions!
4. You can't live a spectacular life of freedom and abundance!
5. You can't build a very successful brand without a degree!

6. You can't become a high-paid consultant — your English is bad, you failed high school!
7. You can't scale your business to generate 7 figures in profits!
8. You can't write another sales letter that generates 8 figures in sales!
9. There's no way you can publish your own book!
10. And you definitely can't become a best-selling author!
11. You can't actually become a consultant/coach!
12. You can't charge $5,000 for an hour of consulting!
13. You can't be a public speaker; it's your number one fear!
14. You can't be an industry leader *and* the number one expert in your field!
15. You can't possibly learn from a billionaire to teach you his business secrets!
16. You can't generate wealth on the Internet!
17. You can't lose half a million dollars and bounce back stronger!
18. It's impossible to invest in real estate and always win!
19. You can't reach true financial independence and live entirely on your own terms!
20. And no matter how hard you try, you can't just have ANYTHING you desire!

And that's just to name a few. You can bet there are a LOT more where they came from. In fact, I just pulled this list from the top of my head to give you an idea of what to expect! But despite how negative these objections were, they all helped me realize one thing, that you'll eventually realize too.

To succeed, you need to stand strong in the face of opposition.

The verdict is clear: Traditional wisdom is failing you and keeping you poor. So next time, when someone says to you, "You can't do that!" You'd better turn and say, "I'm glad you think so. Now watch me!"

These are controversial statements, and most people aren't comfortable facing them. But, I'm dropping serious truth bombs right now. Conventional business wisdom that you hear from your school days right up into adulthood is *designed* to stop you from reaching your potential and breaking into the upper tiers of wealth — the 1%. It's also part of a very important lesson I learned from a billionaire mentor of mine. That lesson was: You need to develop an unbreakable sense of superiority.

Now let me ask you a question. Think about the most successful people you admire. Just pick any one person or group of successful people that you want to model yourself after, to reach their level financially.

Now consider this: "Is their self-esteem high? Or is it low?"

The answer is, they have towering self-esteem, without exception. They kick their lower self to the curb and attack each day with the confidence of a lion! I have *never* met a highly successful person with low self-respect, self-confidence, or self-esteem.

They simply don't exist. Why?

Because **soaring self-esteem is the foundation of all wildly successful people.**

"Every problem is a gift without problems we would not grow."

-Tony Robbins

FIFTEEN

The Eight Attributes Of A Successful Business

Many business owners and would-be entrepreneurs read lots of articles in respected publications about what makes a business successful. These articles frequently talk about various characteristics, like tenacity, but seldom do they discuss the fundamental reason entrepreneurs are successful and what motivates them to take the risks necessary to achieve greatness.

That reason is simple: making their dream money. Everyone has a unique definition of what that is. For some people, that's $100,000 per year. For others, that's $1million. Above all, though, your dream money amount should be more than you can make right now. All too often, entrepreneurs take risks, work long hours, and wind up making the same or less than they could have made working a job.

Think about the businesses most people start. They go into the restaurant business with high overheads, or they drive an Uber, which pays next to nothing. They invest so much time and effort into their companies, all so they can make small sums of money.

With all the time that they spend working on their business, they could probably get a "regular" job and make the same amount of money on an hourly basis.

You have to ask yourself: Why?

There are a plethora of answers to this question, but I believe that they just follow others, and there is an illusion of control. People like the feeling of "being the boss," and everyone is all too happy to sell them that vision. The banks are so glad to lend money since it makes them money, governments are keen to provide some level of capital since it makes them pro-small business. It's a path well-trodden, even though 80% of these businesses fail within the first five years.

In reality, though, many of these entrepreneurs make little money, given all the time they put in. They've traded their day job boss for another, more nightmarish boss — creditors, the taxman, and the necessity to put food on their plate.

How Do You Achieve Your Dream Level of Income?

The best businesses have eight attributes that make them successful:

1. Owners and workers invest in skill development
2. Fantastic marketing abilities and an increased number of leads
3. Add more Vvlue, giving them what they need
4. Increase your transaction value, get more money
5. Being financially prepared
6. Following up on what works and throwing away what doesn't

7. Trying new and different things
8. Being adaptable and willing to change

If the business you build has these eight characteristics, you are putting yourself on the path to success. Remember that the goal of your business is to make you your dream levels of money. You have to be willing to take risks, adapt, and strategize to grow your business to the levels you want.

The Importance of Goals in Business

Remember, your business needs to support your dreams and your aspirations for life. If it isn't doing that, then it's not worth your time.

Consider the following story.

A man travels back in time and wants to showcase how great modern life is. He meets up with a fisher, and he goes on and on about how significant the advances are. The angler listens, intrigued by what the man is saying. Eventually, they start talking about money.

The man tells the fisherman that the future world is so amazing because he can go to a trade school and learn amazing things.

The fisherman asks, "What happens next?"

He says that you can then get a good job and you can work that job until you retire.

The fisherman says, "What's retirement?"

He explains that it's when you can do whatever you want. After working 40 years for a company, you can get on a boat and fish all day if you wish to do so.

The fisherman looks puzzled and asks, "That's what I do all day now. Why is your way better? I get to fish all day now, and I didn't have to work 40 years for someone else to fish!"

The man thinks about it. In reality, he doesn't have a great answer to that question.

Most people don't. They don't have an answer to that question because their monetary goals aren't in line with their career. They're running on the treadmill, hoping to become rich someday. The thing is that if it has zero chance of making the money you want, then it won't work. Ever.

If you dream of driving a Lamborghini, working a minimum wage job for 40 years will not get you there. You can hustle all you want, but you won't ever achieve your goal. You need to learn to make money on your terms!

As discussed above, the goal of your business should be to provide you with your dream levels of money. There are three sub-goals within that:

1. Immediate Cash: You want to make cash right now. Your business should be funding your lifestyle desires in some short-term horizon. Gambling on some big payoff in three years seldom works. You want a payoff now so you can start living the life you want.
2. Monthly Income: Your business should be making you a comfortable income so you can pay your bills.
3. Future Money: Ideally, at some point, you'd be able to cash out and sell your business in the future.

Remember, the goal of your business should be to make you wealthy. If your business isn't currently doing that and it has no hope of ever doing that, it's time to rethink your current strategy!

Focus on the eight characteristics of successful businesses, hone your skills, and make the money you've always dreamed of and deserve!

"The question is not are you worthy enough to reach your goals, the question is are your goals worthy enough of you?"

- Napoleon Hill

SIXTEEN

Your Only Two Commodities [Time And Energy]

This is such an essential concept that I gave it its own chapter to explain it in more detail. If you recall, I introduced this truth to you in the very introduction to this book!

After I started becoming a master trainer in Neuro-Linguistic Programming, I began to study neuroscience and quantum physics in order to become a board member. In my research, I came across this idea that we have only two true commodities in life: time and energy.

The world is reflecting upon us. And the real power of the 1%ers comes through that truth. If you master your time and energy, you master the life of the 1%.

Then, you dominate the marketplace and your competition. Because it's not only discipline but mastery in itself. It cannot be achieved through discipline, but rather, through a deep integration inside of you.

It requires a full mindset of understanding the essential elements of life: where I am going to live, where I am going to eat, how and where I am going to spend my time. And once you have the mindset of making decisions based around these 2 commodities, you become an unstoppable force.

This is when no competition, no recession, no challenge in the marketplace can stop you. This is the secret and red pill of this book. If you look around at your life, you will see just how everything has been designed around you, consuming your time and energy.

The average person in America spends 60–80 hours in traffic or commuting to work because he/she can't live close to work, for whatever reason. This has all been designed by our society. All so that the average person remains average, while someone on the top controls 99% of the world's time and energy.

Once you master this, you are no longer in control of anyone, but you do become the co-creator of your life.

When I was young, my dad used to say to me, "Do you think we are made of money?" And this limiting belief controlled most of our reality. We were told what we were meant to do with our time and energy: We were meant to go to school, find a job, save our pennies, then when we got old and were about to die, use all those pennies to save our lives (especially as in the third world country where I grew up, there weren't any real insurance plans).

We held firm to the limiting belief that we could never be rich or successful, because that was reserved for bad people. We were told how money was bad, and evil, and how it was safer to stay poor for life.

When I grew up and moved to New York City, I realized that money could only expand who you truly are. That it doesn't make you good, and it cannot make you evil. It merely expands what you are already working with before you have it. It expands who you already are.

Money can get you an Uber when it's twenty-five degrees outside, and you're in the middle of nowhere, and the subway line isn't working.

I realized how money could help me hire people who were jobless and invest in hospitals, clinics, orphanages, and so much more. And yes, money can give you accessibility — to grow further and learn more.

Because, like I said, we have only two commodities: time and energy. And in order to learn, grow, and evolve, you need those commodities. And you can only buy those commodities even more when you have more wealth.

"We cannot solve our problems with the same thinking we used when we created them."

-Albert Einstein

SEVENTEEN

The Power Of Being Broke

I remember when I was broke, desperate, and hungry. I was hungry for more. I was hungry for success. The power I gained from being broke was the beginning of testing and accelerating my potential.

At a very young age, I was deported from a communist country for being an entrepreneur Spiritual Advisor, and I was moved to Europe. Through the help of someone who previously worked at the U.N., I was supported in moving to another country as an underage citizen. I tried several different jobs, and then I started a few online businesses. I was confused as hell. Like most people, I had no life direction.

I wasn't sure what I wanted. By that point, I'd experienced many business failures, and I was up to my eyeballs in debt. My self-esteem was low. Let me tell you — it was NO fun waking up in the middle of the night, worrying about how I was going to pay the bills.

I read *Think & Grow Rich,* but nothing was growing. I just didn't know how I could "influence" my friends to loan me money to pay my bills. Safe to say, I was still confused.

I did all the things that most people do, like buying self-help books and tapes and going to seminars. I did all the things the gurus teach: goal setting, positive thinking, affirmations, visualization — all that stuff. Most of it didn't work for me.

I was still broke. I wasn't making enough money, and I certainly wasn't fulfilling my dream.

That's when I made a discovery that changed my entire life's direction. I stumbled across a book in a used bookstore called *Money Making Secrets* by Jay Abraham. The title appealed to me because all my business failures up until that point had boiled down to one problem: a lack of customers.

I bought the book. I must have read it 6 times in a row. It changed my life. The book revealed to me that there's actually a science to marketing and attracting clients.

And from that point on, I was absolutely hooked on all this marketing stuff. I started buying all the marketing books I could get my hands on. I studied ads and sales letters. I wanted to know what made people tick and what motivated them to buy.

Most people buy magazines to read the articles. I would buy magazines to read the ads. People throw away their junk mail; I read my junk mail before I opened my bills. In fact, I was getting all kinds of junk mail because I purposely ordered stuff from mail-order companies. All so I could see different offers and pitches.

I wanted to be sold to. I came across Rhonda Byrne's *The Secret,* and there I accidentally saw my first mentor, Bob Proctor, in a video where he asked: What do you want? What do you really want? He explained how the programs I was giving myself kept me stuck in my paradigm. From there, I started studying the mind, and as I was studying it, it helped me realize more about why and how I was influencing people as a psychic and how they were finding their success.

So, I started practicing as a Consultant & Coach, to help people in their life and business understand why they couldn't find success. Even that was a huge niche to work in, and I was doing everything, but I was learning what was preventing my clients from succeeding.

When I moved to New York City, I came across Daymond John, and I studied more about business and why people fail. It allowed me to see from a broader perspective. And then I came across many other mentors, including Dr. James. I started to get a clear sense of direction about how life is really 80% mind and 20% mechanics.

I studied the mind through quantum physics, neuroscience, Esoteric, Master Training in NLP, and neuroplasticity. After becoming an American board member of Neuro-Linguistic Programming, I found the Magic Pill people needed.

You see, I spent over $836,000 to find those answers, and it clearly made sense how marketing works and why people buy and why they do not. How big companies have been using these secrets for years, but no one ever wants to share or talk about it to 95%.

This is when I decided to start training entrepreneurs who wanted to be successful. And one after the other, they started seeing massive results in their sales and profits. Learn more about it through my free class at www.quantumastercoach.com/freemasterclass.

"I believe the last thing I read at night will likely manifest when I'm sleeping. You become what you think about the most"

- Daymond John

EIGHTEEN

The Power Of Your Social Assets

Today, you and I are not living in the same economy in which we were born.

The most important asset in today's world? At this point, you may be thinking of assets such as land and property, equipment, or possibly a college education, but the answer in business is real genuine fans.

I know of various individuals and business profiles on social media that have hundreds of thousands or even millions of followers, but there are two unfortunate realities that these people are facing. Firstly, these followers are fake. They aren't genuine people who have bought into the brand and solutions that are on offer, and as a result (the second unfortunate reality), these people with fake followers aren't generating success. Some are even broke.

If you deliver on your expectations to your target audience with great solutions and great online content, then your genuine fan base will grow — and they will help your brand go viral so that others get to know you and will want to be associated with you as well.

Having fans who want to tell the rest of the world about how incredible you are is the most important marketing asset anyone can have. Viral marketing (also described as word of mouth or referrals) means that your loyal fans are growing your business for you (and without you having to throw money at marketing activities to convince people who don't know you that you are credible). If you don't have these loyal fans who love your brand and tone and style, then it's almost impossible to survive and grow your business over the long term.

The best way to create this buzz with your fans and potential new customers? Make sure you are present on all marketing channels — especially online.

So, it's not just about getting attention online. It's important to engage with fans who trust your brand and love what you do. Getting the attention of people who aren't your target market means leaving money on the table. Targeting the right people with the right content, however, is the best way to turn a marketing activity into large profits.

The key to scaling your business for success is to turn followers into lead generators for sales. Setting up strategic partnerships and collaborations with followers means that they are generating business for you, but this doesn't happen overnight. Givers gain, and the more you 'give' and reward your fans, the more likely they are going to help you 'gain.' Imagine it as an emotional bank account.

When you add value to your fans, you are depositing into the account. You have to make deposits first. You can't withdraw from the account if it's empty! Fill the emotional bank account up, and you will have plenty to draw from.

One of the biggest mistakes brands make on social media is to sell, sell, sell without having first delivered something of value — something that helps build trust with their target audience. If all you do is sell without adding value, what makes you different? Why should anyone buy from you when there are so many other businesses offering the same or similar solutions?

Add value, stand out, and build trust with the right people. It's the only way to truly thrive.

"Rich people believe 'I create my life.' Poor people believe 'Life happens to me."'

- T. Harv Eker

NINETEEN

The Power Of Your Personal Branding

For anyone doing business in 2020, building a personal brand has never been more important. Whether you are an entrepreneur, freelancer, or working your way up the corporate ladder, the competition has never been fiercer.

The key to differentiating yourself from others is to build a personal brand that is recognizable. Your personal brand distinguishes you from competitors and helps build trust with your followers that turns into long-lasting relationships.

Nowadays, people are more inclined to do business with someone they know and trust. If you can leave a lasting impression in the minds of your audience, they will continue to want to do business with you.

Also, with the rise of the Internet and social media, there are a lot of distractions out there. One way to cut through all the noise is to build a strong and solid reputation. By creating a personal brand based on transparency, honesty, and showing who you truly are, you can quickly and easily build trust. This is something that not many people take the time to craft.

People connect with people, not companies. Your personal brand represents your company's brand, and you can leverage it to increase exposure and attract more customers to your company. In the end, however, your personal brand is your own.

When you have a great personal brand, your business may change or even die, but your personal brand will not. Your personal brand will transition with you to any business. The truth is, people do not buy into you because of the product or service you are selling; rather, they buy in because of who you are.

Personal branding is a safety net. It is a recession-proof formula for your career.

Money follows attention, and when you have a great personal brand, you can get attention from a massive audience, especially on social media. This is because an effective personal media brand tells a story that connects people to you and, as they say, "facts tell, stories sell."

Your story is such an important part of your personal brand.

It gives you leverage to hook people with your story and offer. With this, you can scale your business and start making 7, 8, or even 9 figures!

People have come to me for help who have 10 or even 12 million followers but are completely broke. This is because they have nothing to sell. It's not followers that bring you money, it's how you position yourself with your personal media brand.

With a great personal media brand, you don't need 10 million followers. You only need 100 or so diehard, rabid fans. When you have this, as I said before, they will do your marketing for you.

If you want to see top-notch personal branding in action, there are so many great examples to look at. People like Apple's Steve Jobs, Facebook's Mark Zuckerberg, Alibaba's Jack Ma, and author J.K. Rowling are all masters of personal branding. Maybe the best example though are the reality TV stars-turned-moguls, Kylie Jenner and Kim Kardashian.

They are true masters of personal branding. They have built a massive following for their personal brands over the last decade. They have both leveraged their audience to launch products and sell millions of units.

Do these entrepreneurs have the best products? Maybe not, but people buy them because of the brand. This is an added benefit of having a strong personal brand. You can justify charging a premium price for your product and services.

You already have a personal brand, even if you've never thought about building one. Don't believe me? Google yourself! See what the results show.

Now, it's just a matter of leading your brand in the direction you want it to go. You need to define what you want your brand to represent and your audience. After that, all you need to do is start building real relationships with real people and build your brand every day like a habit.

At its core, your brand is your reputation. It is essential for your business, your career, and your success. Those who can understand how to yield the power of your networks and brand will achieve significantly more than the average person.

Just remember, it takes years and lots of effort to build your personal brand to where you want it, but only one slip up to tarnish it.

"Financial freedom is freedom from fear."

- Robert Kiyosaki

TWENTY

Your Invitation

I truly hope that my experiences help to speed up the learning process for you. Instead of feeling stressed or overwhelmed, you can do things quicker and better with much fewer mistakes. The advice I am providing is focused on proven practices to help you achieve greater success.

I am sure that right about now you're probably shaking your head with too much information, which is completely understandable. The concepts I've laid out here took me over 15 years to discover, learning from different mentors at different level of my life.

It took me many times of failures and learnings.

So, where to begin? Here are the steps I recommend taking:

1. Master a skill set 100% fully. Most people master 40% and keep adding more skills without fully mastering any of them.
2. Add value first before asking for money.
3. Take the actions that get results for you and your prospect. These results are the starting point for long-term success for your business.

4. Make a difference! What value you are delivering to the marketplace and what you offer is an opportunity to change the world and the lives of many people. Take the opportunity to make a difference.

I have spent a lot of time researching, testing, and analyzing results to see what works — as well as writing this book based on what is proven to work. I truly hope you have found reading this book a valuable investment. As much value as this book is, however, it cannot replace face-to-face support, and I'm happy to personally help further, including support from my team.

If you would like to take your business to the next level with my support, then you are invited to get in touch or attend one of my events. Just click here to get started: www.quantumastercoach.com/freemasterclass.

Contribution is important to success and, at this stage, it's worth recognizing that you have taken the next step beyond personal growth by acting to help others and to make a difference in their lives. As you use the life lessons and experience you have acquired to help others, you will feel more fulfilled and happier in life, knowing that you are making a difference to people on a daily basis.

Selling might not be your thing, but it's a fundamental activity for any person or business to succeed. Many people don't realize that selling is something we do every day, consciously or subconsciously.

Whether it's convincing our partner which new car to buy, prompting the kids to do the right thing, explaining to the boss why we should have a promotion, or something else — we are always selling — and knowing that you are adding value to people's lives and being paid is a huge reward.

Stay focused on the process of creating value, growing followers, and generating leads, and you will be rewarded, not just with great profits, but with the satisfaction of a fulfilled life!

"If you get up in the morning and think the future is going to be better, it is a bright day. Otherwise, it's not."

- Elon Musk

Conclusion

Your most important asset is not Money, Cars and Houses, but your Expert Skill Set, Courage, Commitment, Persistence, and Humility.

-John Qreshi

Where *do I go from here?*

Thank you for taking the time to read this book. I want to congratulate you for taking the first important step to success! We have covered a lot in this book, but it's not possible to cover all of the details in one publication. You can also access a range of materials, including the detailed steps on how to build and scale your business by creating social capital and how to use your greatest assets for even better results.

Take your business and knowledge to the next level by visiting my site: www.quantumastercoach.com/freeclass

Now, don't just apply those habits, integrate them! I have truly given you the keys to unleash your success, wealth, and significance. I have shared with you how I think, the lessons I have learned in life, and my business views.

And now that you have achieved the right mindset and acquired the appropriate tools, you now have the keys to unleash and become more of what you are truly capable of. You are the master key to unleashing yourself, whether what you seek is more freedom, more success, more money, or anything you can be in control of.

Does it all stop here?

Now that you have read this book, you have two choices: Procrastinate and get busy doing what you have always done or take yourself and your business to the next level using the insights you have gained from this book. I hope you will take the latter option and massively grow your business using your potential and the new skills you acquire along the journey.

If you want to be a part of the small group of people that are highly successful, then don't stop at just reading this book. Take action and continue by taking the next steps to success.

I feel great pride and satisfaction in knowing that I can also make a difference in your life and would love to work with you on your journey to success. Make sure to connect with me on social media, and don't forget to check out my events and training sessions that are available to help you.

And remember — stay focused, strive to learn, and take positive action to get results!

I would like to end this with three questions to ask yourself:

1. Who am I to dream again?
2. Who am I to live the life I want?
3. Who am I to produce the results I want?

This is the end.

Made in the USA
Monee, IL
04 November 2026

67386098R10115